Funny Stories
FROM MOSTLY
North Dakota
Schools

Other Books by Kevin Kremer:

*Captain Grant Marsh:
The GreatestSteamboatman in History*

A Kremer Christmas Miracle

Spaceship Over North Dakota

Saved by Custer's Ghost

The Blizzard of the Millennium

When it Snows in Sarasota

Santa's Our Substitute Teacher

Are You Smarter Than a Flying Gator

Maggie's Christmas Miracle

The Year Our Teacher Won the Super Bowl

The Most Amazing Halloween Ever

Are You Smarter Than a Flying Teddy

Angel of the Prairie

The Worst Day of School EVER—Do-Over

Valentine Shmellentine

Funny Stories
From Mostly
North Dakota Schools

by Kevin Kremer

Published by Kremer Publishing
2020
P.O. Box 1385
Osprey, FL 34229-1385

www.KevinKremerBooks.com

Copyright © 2020 by Kevin Kremer

Kremer Publishing
P.O. Box 1385
Osprey, FL 34229-1385
(941)-822-0549

Visit us on the web! **KevinKremerBooks.com**

All rights reserved.

ISBN: 978-1-7333492-5-3

First Edition

Book design by Elisabeth Arena.

Without limiting the rights under copyright reserved above, no part of this publication may be reproduced, stored in, or introduced into a retrieval system, or transmitted, in any form, or by any means (electronic, mechanical, photocopying, recording, or otherwise) without the prior written permission of both the copyright owner and the above publisher of this book.

This book is dedicated to all the people who have ever made me laugh. Laughter is truly the best medicine—and it doesn't require a prescription!

Special Thanks

*To Elisabeth Arena for her great work designing the book.

*To everyone who took the time to contribute a story to this book.

*To God, country, family, friends—and the Pittsburgh STEELERS!

Introduction

Kevin Kremer grew up in Mandan, North Dakota, and he taught in North Dakota Schools, so compiling a book of Funny Stories from mostly North Dakota Schools was not that difficult and a lot of fun. Heck, all seven of his brothers and sisters were educators at one time, and he knew he could think of at least 25 funny stories of his own, so he didn't need much more than that for a book.

Then he decided to place a notice on a few North Dakota Facebook pages and hopefully get some more funny stories. After several months, he had enough material for a book.

He decided to break the book up into four major parts:

Part 1: Stories from many different contributors.

Part 2: Stories from Joni Magstadt, a second grade teacher who had taken the time to write down many cute, funny stories during her final years of teaching.

Part 3: Stories from Kevin's good friend Duane Roth, who taught 35 years at Pioneer Elementary School in Bismarck.

Part 4: Fifty of Kevin Kremer's own stories as a student, a teacher, and author visiting schools all over the place.

We hope you enjoy this book. We have a feeling the stories will remind you of some of the things that happened in your schools.

CONTENTS

Part 1: Funny Stories from a Bunch of People

1. I'm ready to explain MY problem! —Patrick Kremer........3
2. Oh! Mr. Kremer! —Patrick Kremer 5
3. The Napkins—Paulette Bullinger........6
4. The Spelling Bee—Dewey Reinert........10
5. Meet Mr. Broten—Kelly Kremer........12
6. First Window Story—Phil Kambeitz........15
7. Second Window Story—Phil Kambeitz........17
8. Jaw-Dropping Coincidence—Mark D. Olmsted........19
9. Don't Use This as a Crutch—Michael Stroker........21
10. How Many North Dakota Kids Had This Happen to Them?—Pamela Wyckoff........24
11. That's Just WRONG—Joyce Poppe........25
12. Going Batty at Pioneer—Kurt Weinberg........28
13. Bright Idea—Robin Ladd........32
14. What Were You Doing in My Underwear Drawer?—Keith Kremer........35
15. Who Let the Goat Out?—Keith Kremer........36
16. Skip—Keith Kremer........37
17. Funny and Heartwarming too—Keith Kremer........38
18. Technology—Oh My!—Carol J. Baillie........40
19. What About the Remainder?—Carol J. Baillie........43
20. Roly-Poly—Carol J. Baillie........43
21. The Donut Tree—Kristin Small........44
22. Oops!—Mike Grotte........46
23. There is No Blizzard!—Michael L. Kremer........47
24. Arly's Little Trick—Michael L. Kremer........48
25. Paper Bag on the Desk—Karen Smink........50
26. Lesson FAIL—Karen Smink........52

27. I told Jeff—Anonymous...53
28. A Stinky Story—Lee Russell Brown..............................55
29. Bug Busters in South Carolina—Anonymous...............58
30. Riding the Struggle Bus—Jennifer Hayes....................60
31. You Never Want THAT Taken Out—Darlene Paulson..61
32. Aunt Dolores Had to Sit Under the Teacher's Desk—Dolores Kremer Wells..62
33. Tissue Flowers—Joan Nelson Auch...............................63
34. Line Up for Your Shots—Carlene Fitterer.....................65
35. How Long?—Carlene Fitterer..66
36. I Was Buying Drugs—Anonymous..................................67
37. Hup, Two, Three, Four—about (losing) face!—Carolyn King 68
38. Stolen Lunch—Mary Baird...71
39. Tying Shoes—Carlene Bahm..73
40. I Need an Ambulance—Anonymous...............................74
41. That Jump Rope Didn't Stop Us—Ed Trejo...................75
42. The Pretty Dress—Norene Sandberg..............................76
43. Watch Out for Those Brainstorms—Peggy Kopp.........77
44. Our Kid Will Pay for the Gas—Sue Triska....................79
45. How can you beat a steak?—Sue Triska........................80
46. Who Let the Dogs Out?—Sue Triska..............................80
47. Clearing the Lunch Table!—Wayne Triska....................82
48. I swallowed my eye!—Wayne Triska..............................83
49. I can insert that prosthetic eye!—Wayne Triska..........83
50. Right-side up—Wayne Triska..84

Part 2: Funny Stories from Joni Magstadt's Second Grade Class 86

Part 3: Funny Stories from Duane Roth

1. First Words Spoken..168
2. You Mean a Big Thing Like YOU?......................168
3. Sometimes You Can't Help Yourself....................169
4. The Old Mimeograph machine............................170
5. You Can't Beat Head Cheese................................170
6. You're FIRED!..171
7. I Patiently Wait..171
8. Winnie Hoersch Fun...172
9. He Wrote a Whole Page..172
10. It Was a Delicate Situation Wrestling a Girl......173
11. Minister Referee..173
12. Wayne Triska Story...174
13. Bubble Wrap..174
14. Please Pass the Mouth Wash..............................175
15. Chalkboard Wisdom...175
16. The Big Words..175
17. The F-Word...176
18. Ginny Eck..176
19. Donald Dook...177
20. Go Get Her!...177
21. The Talking Calculator.......................................178
22. Money Was Tight..179
23. English Teacher Fun...179
24. You Deserve a Ticket..180
25. Just Jump!..181
26. The Hand and the Trash Can.............................181
27. That's Warming Up Your Car!...........................182
28. The Good Lord Will Do It.................................183
29. Terrific Dean Turner...183
30. The Simple Things Can Be the Best..................184
31. Is it a Real Diamond?...184
32. Where's Waldo?...185

33. Doing an experiment on the professor!......186
34. The kid REALLY got into it!......187

Part 4: Funny Stories from Kevin Kremer

1. You've GOT to be KIDDING me!......190
2. No More English Leather!......191
3. Some Records Were Meant to be Broken......192
4. Pennies from Heaven......192
5. The Tear Gas Incident of 1964......193
6. The Booming Voice of Lefty Faris!......194
7. I'll Give You $10......197
8. What is this SHEET?......198
9. Fake Classroom Visitor from Australia......199
10. Pull-up GEESE......201
11. The Blizzard of 1997......202
12. Santa is Watching......206
13. Describe that guy that just came in......208
14. Booger-Picker......209
15. April Fools at Highland Acres......209
16. Cross-Country Wrong Way......210
17. Band-Aid on the Face......211
18. That's My Daddy!......212
19. Hey! I wrote the book!......214
20. Most Surprising Teacher Christmas Gift......214
21. Bend Down and Touch Your Ankles......215
22. Half-Court Shot......217
23. Fake Seizure......218
24. Look at Aunt Bertha......219
25. All it takes is one word!......221
26. Behind the back......223
27. Mathketball......224
28. Math Football Game......225
29. Money Tree......226

30. Poolside Party..................226
31. It's Polka Time..................228
32. The Ghost Radio in the Gym..................228
33. Comedy Relief at the Formal School Evaluation........230
34. My First "B" ever..................231
35. Kremer Kash..................234
36. Peanut Butter Sandwiches..................235
37. Scavenger Hunt in Rugby..................236
38. Rhyme all the Time..................237
39. The Band-Aid Class..................237
40. I Think That's Larry Bird!..................238
41. 50 Below! No Problem!..................239
42. Mr. Bubble Visits..................240
43. STEELERS Fan for Life..................241
44. Upside Down Argument..................242
45. Can't you even beat my student manager!?..................243
46. Most Embarrassing Junior High Memory..................244
47. Three Johns..................245
48. Uncle Jack..................245
49. No way, Jamie!..................247
50. Kevin #1 and Kevin #2..................249

Part 1:
Funny Stories from a Bunch of People

1: I'm ready to explain MY problem!

Patrick Kremer
Teacher and administrator for 35 years, retired
Marshalltown, Iowa
I love being a Grandpa!

My first year of teaching in Ellendale, North Dakota, was a year to remember. I was the only sixth grade teacher in town. I had 36 students, and they were a wonderful group! Six years later, they invited me back to Ellendale to speak at their Senior Banquet.

I'll never forget the day I gave them a scare and a laugh in the same minute. I loved teaching math, and one of the techniques I learned while a student in Mandan from my wonderful math teachers Mr. Coats and Mr. Lundstrom was having my students do math problems at the chalkboard and standing at the board to explain the problem to the class.

On this particular day, I stood at the back of the room. As I asked the students at the board if they were ready to explain their problems, I stepped backward toward a folding table against the wall and sat on the table. The legs on the table were not securely locked, and I went crashing to the floor! The room went silent, and all eyes turned to the back of the room. I slowly picked myself off the floor and looked at the hole on the top of the table. I turned slowly to the class and reported, "Well, I'm ready to explain MY problem!" They burst into laughter!

2: Oh! Mr. Kremer!—Patrick Kremer

My last job in education was associate superintendent in Marshalltown, Iowa. I had served there as an elementary school teacher in grades three to six, a middle school associate principal, and an elementary principal. On the last day of school one year, I received a call from one of our middle school principals. He reported that a parent was on her way to my office, very upset, as he had suspended her child from school on the last day due to her involvement in a cafeteria food fight. The parent was NOT happy!

Sure enough, my phone rang and the receptionist informed me there was a parent to see me. I made my way to the front office to meet the parent. I came around the corner and recognized the parent immediately, and it was obvious in the eyes of the parent that she recognized me as well. Very sheepishly, her first words were, "Oh! Mr. Kremer." And I replied, "Hi, Robin."

This was a parent who had been a student in one of my first classes when I was a classroom teacher. All anger disappeared from her eyes, and she smiled. "Come in my office," I said. "Let's talk about what we want your child to learn from this problem today." And we did.

3: The Napkins

Paulette Bullinger
Wife, Mom, Grandma
Photographer, Writer
Bismarck, North Dakota

In the 1960s, I grew up in a small community that had a country grade school. My first eight years of school were in the Bonanza School District of Morton County, North Dakota. The school was located in Huff.

Those days, very little was taught in country schools regarding *women's health*. In fact, nothing was taught that I recall, even though girls attending at that time would range in age from six to fifteen. These subjects were the responsibility of a mother, an older sister, or even discussions among the older girls on the playground.

Not having an older sister to hear such discussions and too shy to join in the *big girl's group*, I knew absolutely nothing about the physical changes I would experience in a few short years of my twelfth birthday, the year I was a sixth grader in our school of 20 students.

Our country school consisted of the typical *little white schoolhouse* design. One large room held all eight grades. In the front of this room was the teacher's large wooden desk facing the students. Blackboards and maps were on the front wall behind her with a small coal stove in the corner. There was a small library and textbooks on the rear wall, and one wall had large windows facing the playground in easy view of the teacher at her desk.

The school had no running water or indoor bathroom facilities. The entrance to the school was our cloakroom where we left our lunch pails, and it also contained a large Red Wing crock for drinking water with a dipper for us to share. The water was carried from a nearby pump by the older boys. There were two outhouses at the rear of the school grounds, one for boys and one for girls.

One day, during recess, our teacher, Mrs. Schmidt called all the girls from fifth through eighth grade to come inside and gather around her desk. Pointing to an open drawer in her desk, she whispered "Now, you young ladies can bring your napkins to school and place them in this drawer, so when you are in need of one, please take one of your own." I thought the request was peculiar, but Mrs. Schmidt was strict, so I thought I better follow the order.

The next morning at school, I presented Mrs. Schmidt with my package of napkins, beautifully designed by Scot towels. It was a package of 100 I took from the grocery store my parents operated in Huff. She accepted the package and slowly placed them in the bottom drawer with an overly big smile on her face for Mrs. Schmidt!

That evening, Mother took me into her bedroom, closed the door, and shared some of the most unbelievable and shocking anatomy information I had ever heard! She also said, "I hope this explains why Daddy moves the Kotex boxes back to the medicine cabinet in the store." You see, my job growing up in the back of the store was to stock and dust the shelves. When the freight truck would come in, it seemed as though I was constantly reorganizing the napkins to be with the paper towels and dinner napkins, only to get up in the morning to find them moved.

This offers a humorous glimpse into the way things were when I was twelve.

4: The Spelling Bee

Dewey Reinert
Letter carrier since 1994
U. S. Postal Service
Bismarck, North Dakota

I was in the fourth grade at Dorothy Moses Elementary School during the 1980-81 schoolyear. There were four classrooms of fourth grade students, each consisting of about 24 students. The teachers had decided to have a *spelling bee* among all of the students.

I considered myself a pretty good speller, and I was looking forward to this event. I can't remember how well I did, what the exact rules were, or which classroom or student won the competition. I doubt if many other students or teachers that were present that day can recall any of those facts either.

However, there are a few of us that will never forget an incident that occurred that day. We were all lined up waiting for our turns to see what word would be called out for us to spell. A boy from another classroom was asked to spell *North Dakota*. Most of the students and teachers quietly giggled when he was given this word. The boy had no idea why everyone was laughing when he attempted to spell it. We all had our undivided attention focused on him, and the boy couldn't figure out why. I know he spelled *North* correctly, but he misspelled *Dakota*. All of us laughed even louder when he spelled it incorrectly. Even the teachers were laughing!

It wasn't because we thought it was easy to spell. The reason we were all laughing was due to the fact that the boy was wearing a shirt that had **North Dakota** printed on it at least 10 times in large letters!

5: MEET MR. BROTEN

KELLY KREMER
YOUNGEST OF EIGHT
EDUCATOR/SWIM COACH
GOPHER AND STEELER FAN

It was our first day of class, sixth grade year. Finally we were the so-called big kids of Central Elementary School in Mandan, North Dakota. But my friends and I were more anxious than excited on this day. There was a new teacher in our school. Sixth grade this particular year would be taught by a male teacher, Mr. Spencer J. Broten.

We had been together, my friends and I, since the

very beginning. A string of five female teachers in a row, and while we certainly didn't have the greatest reputation for good behavior, we had survived and made it here to the top of the elementary ladder. But what would this year's teacher be like? How would having a male teacher differ from having a female teacher? In the world today, no big deal, but back then, this was big news, and somewhat scary to my friends and me.

Shortly before the bell, Mr. Broten entered the room. I am not sure how tall he was or how built he was, but he was BIG to us! He strolled to the front of the room. He turned to face the class. We were all looking at each other, mumbling things that sixth graders mumble, but in retrospect we were simply burning off some nervous energy.

The bell rang. We were still creating chatter and noise when Mr. Broten addressed the class for the first time. I can still see and hear him as if it was yesterday. ... Rocking back and forth from heel to toes, hands in his pockets, he says, "My name is Mr. Broten. I have only one rule. There will be no talking!"

You could have heard a pin drop. My friends and I

were wide-eyed and looking around at one another as if we weren't sure we all heard the same thing. *No talking? Was he serious?*

Without missing a beat, he lifted up the map and projector screen that covered the chalkboard in the front of the room to reveal the sentence THERE WILL BE NO TALKING. *He was serious.* I wondered to myself which of us would get in trouble first. This was going to be a long, miserable, and obviously quiet year.

Mr. Broten loosened up eventually. He became an all-time favorite of mine. He inspired me to like school, and I began thinking about being a teacher because of him. He let my friends and me know months later that he had been warned about us because of what our prior teachers had said, and he knew he had to make a strong statement on day one. He *did*, and I have never forgotten it, or him.

6: First Window Story

PHIL KAMBEITZ
RETIRED SCHOOL SOCIAL WORKER AND STILL SUBSTITUTING
WRITING FAMILY HISTORY, STORIES, AND GENEALOGY
BISMARCK, ND

Mary Wendt was a student in the Bismarck Public Schools. Her father was Superintendent Simle. She told me the story of a year-end caper at Bismarck High School.

Mary indicated that a boy in her class had been suffering through senior English class for almost nine months and felt as though he needed to liven things up a bit. On a hot day in May the windows were opened to bring in some fresh air since during those times there was no air conditioning in schools.

Class was held on the third floor of Bismarck High. In the middle of class the mischievous young man left his desk and jumped up on the window sill. He announced loudly to the class, "I can't take this anymore!" With the startled class and teacher looking on, he leapt from that third story window!

The panicked teacher ran to the window, thinking the worst. ... She saw her student bouncing up and down. He had an accomplice who had placed the physical education trampoline below the window.

7: Second Window Story—Phil Kambeitz

Many years later, Rick Heidt was assistant principal at Bismarck High School. He told a story of pre-air conditioning times when windows could still be opened and closed.

On this particular nice day a student left class to use the bathroom. However, rather than going all the way down the hall to use the proper facilities, he noticed an open window overlooking the parking lot. He started to pee out the window when he noticed a traveling teacher walking across the parking lot on the way to the building. Although she looked up to see him, he maintained his composure and even waved at her while continuing to relieve himself.

She reported the incident to the assistant principal. She described the student, and the principal immediately called the suspected student's classroom, requesting he come to his office.

Before coming down to the office, the student traded shirts with a friend. In the office the student denied that it was him and confronted the assistant principal as to why he was so sure it was him. He asked the principal if the boy was wearing a plaid shirt like his.

The principal said, "No, he wasn't wearing plaid, but you are the only boy in school today who has a cast on his left arm, the arm you used to wave at our teacher from that window."

8: Jaw-Dropping Coincidence

Mark D. Olmsted, O.D.
Optometrist
Fergus Falls, Minnesota
I Don't Call Patients "Honey"

I was attending school at Hughes Junior High School in Bismarck. On a morning in the spring of 1976 I had something in my eye. My mom took me to the St. Alexius ER, and luckily there was an eye care professional on call to address the situation. Being a 14-year-old-boy with slightly long hair, I did not appreciate Dr. Reichert calling me *honey* but he fixed the issue. A nurse put a great big pressure patch on my eye after which my mom took me back to Hughes.

When I walked into the office, I told Principal Yonker that I needed a late slip. His *dad-joke* response was, "What you really need is a poke in the eye."

I was about 15 minutes late for my first period eighth grade English class taught by Mr. Sailer (pronounced Sigh-ler). The subject of the day was the Edgar Allen Poe story, "The Black Cat." The door to the room was in the front so I would need to walk right toward the teacher at the podium in front of the whole class.

As I quietly entered the room with my late pass, Mr. Sailer was just talking about the part in Poe's story where the drunk character was gouging out the eye of the black cat with a knife. When he finished the sentence, he turned toward me, walking into the room, wearing that huge eyepatch. His eyes got super-wide and he did an almost cartoonish jaw drop. The whole class fell to a silence that I've never *heard* since. Nobody even breathed as I nonchalantly found my seat. The look on that teacher's face is a memory that I will never forget.

9: Don't Use This as a Crutch

MICHAEL STROKER
FEDEX RETIREE
SALISBURY, MARYLAND
PRAISE GOD!

In the spring of 1968, I was a member of the tennis team at John Carroll High School in Bel Air, Maryland. As my teammates and I were finishing up practice, a good buddy of mine, Jim, came hobbling up to the tennis courts. Surprised to see Jim in that condition, I went over to him and asked what happened. He told me it was a knee injury from a collision at lacrosse practice. I asked if I could try out his crutches to see what it was like, and he said, "Sure."

I proceeded to hop around on the crutches playfully, only to fall and land awkwardly. Everybody, including me, was laughing until I realized I had severely sprained an ankle. You guessed it—I wound up on crutches of my own.

My tennis coach, Mr. Pons, who happened to also be my physical education teacher, was not amused, knowing that I would not be able to contribute to the success of the team. So, the next morning I negotiated my way down the hall to phys. ed. class. When I hobbled in, everybody was snickering, knowing the circumstances. Even Mr. Pons had a smirk on his face anticipating my arrival, but he greeted me warmly and asked how I was doing.

Mr. Pons told me to sit in the back of the room where I could lean the crutches against the corner wall so as not to cause any students to trip over them. He had a wickedly funny sense of humor, and my circumstances gave him an opening to share his thoughts. "Mr. Stroker," he proclaimed, pointing at my crutches in the corner, "don't even think about using those sticks as a crutch for being late to class or getting a better grade in phys. ed."

Everybody in class roared with laughter, including

Mr. Pons and me. With some rehab, I was back on the tennis team healthy, and I received a good grade in phys. ed., which Mr. Pons attributed to my focus on recovering from my injury. My friend Jim recovered also and resumed his role as goalie on the lacrosse team.

10: How Many North Dakota Kids Had This Happen to Them?

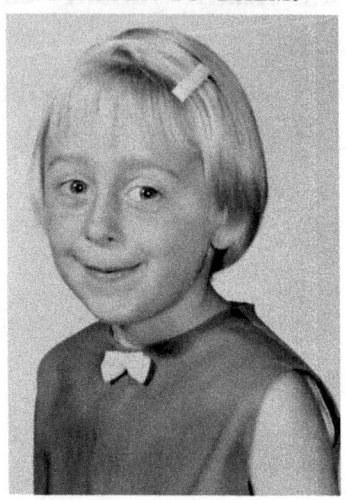

PAMELA WYCKOFF
BORN IN CROSBY, ND TO 3RD GENERATION FARMERS
RETIRED AFTER 31 YEARS FROM UC DAVIS
HAVE A SON AND DAUGHTER IN TURLOCK, CA

Back in 1963, I was in first grade in Riverdale, North Dakota. During recess on a cold winter day, I was having fun on the little merry-go-round. You guessed it! I stuck my tongue on the metal rails. … And you know what happened next—the bell rang and all the kids ran back to class. I didn't show up. My dad, the principal, found me, still on the merry-go-round with my tongue stuck to it. I can't remember exactly how they got my tongue unstuck from that merry-go-round.

11. That's Just **WRONG!**

Joyce Poppe
Minneapolis, Minnesota
Retired elementary teacher

Over the years I had many students in my third grade classroom who were on the autism spectrum. One who really stood out was a boy named Garret. He was a character, to say the least. He had a glass eye, and on one occasion in second grade, he got so upset with his teacher that he took out his glass eye and rolled it across the floor toward her. I vowed that that would never happen in our classroom, and thankfully it did not.

One of my favorite stories about Garret involves his beliefs involving the hierarchy of roles in our school. To Garret, all males were more important than females, no matter what their job was. So our principal, Mr. Anderson, was by far at the top of the ladder. No one was more important in Garret's eyes than Mr. Anderson. The second most important person in our school was Mr. Lee, the physical education teacher, and the third most important person was Larry, our custodian. This was how Garret viewed things, and he was unwavering in that view.

The summer before Garret was in my class, our school district hired a new superintendent, Dr. Larson, who happened to be a woman. One day in October, Dr. Larson was touring our school, and she came into our classroom. I explained to our class that she was our new superintendent of schools. As she was walking around our classroom, she came over to Garett's desk where he was working on an assignment. He looked up at her and said, "Who are you again?" She replied, "I'm Dr. Larson, the new superintendent."

When she saw the puzzled look on Garett's face, she made the mistake of further explaining her role in this way, "I'm Mr. Anderson's boss."

Garret suddenly had a look of horror on his face and shouted, "That's just WRONG!"

Needless to say, I had all I could do to stifle my laugh.

12: Going Batty at Pioneer

Kurt Weinberg
Husband, Dad, Grandpa
Retired after 39 years with Bismarck Public Schools
Bismarck, ND by way of upstate New York

At the end of summer, the week before school is always stressful and full of hard work by teachers preparing for their new classes of students. Everything has to be just right for the kids' arrival the first day of school, and as a result, many teachers put in some late nights at school making final preparations. That was the case one evening at Pioneer Elementary in Bismarck, North Dakota. I was in the gym setting up bulletin boards and prepping equipment for the first day of school, and the school was humming with activity with about five other teachers working in their rooms. My son Luke had offered to come help me with all the work that had to be done.

Luke and I went down the hall to make some copies, and from the end of the hall I hear hollering and wailing, "Weinberg! I'm pinned down behind the copier! There's a bat flying around!"

Ahh! Luke and I make a U-turn and returned to the hallway with tennis racquets and lacrosse sticks in hand to do battle with the little bugger. We put up a great front! Long story short, we rescued Netzer and got her back to her room safely and without incident. She worked behind closed doors the rest of the evening. But the story does not end there!

On opening day the school was abuzz with children, from new little ones attending for the first time, all the way up to the older kids, strutting around with confidence and enjoying renewing friendships and swapping tales of summer adventures. The kindergartners run the full range of readiness. A few walk in confidently, many are quiet, and still others are tearful and grasping at their mom's skirt tails, unwilling to make the break. Point being, the majority are a little fragile this first day of school.

Fast forward to later in the day in my gym. I meet the kinders at the gym door, and they meekly enter, wondering what this whole *gym thing* is all about. For my first few lessons with little ones, I like to have the kinders come in and sit around me on the floor as I try to learn some names and do some simple rhyming and small movement activities. This is by design to make them feel comfortable and not be intimidated by the huge gym.

As I'm leading a song called *Bubblegum*, I catch movement in the air across the gym. ... No! It can't be! No, it is! ... The damn bat is flying around the gym!

Not wanting to draw attention to the flying beast, I move my eyes back to the kids. "Icky Sticky Icky Stick Bubble Gum, Bubble Gum," I continue. Sneaking a look at the flying bat, it begins to make arcs closer and closer to our little group. I can't resist looking up. God, it can't come over and bite one of my kiddos. ... I take a longer look and the unthinkable happens. Three kinders follow my gaze to the bat and scream, "It's a bat flying around!"

Three kids jump in the air and into my lap, holding on for dear life. Twenty-five kinder kids are soon screaming at the top of their lungs, some crying, some frozen in fear, and a few ready to chase our flying friend around the gym.

Eventually I regain control of this hot mess and we evacuate the gym to the hallway just outside the gym. The classroom teacher was a bit surprised when she came to pick up her kids and we were in the hallway rather than in the gym. "Why are you out here, Weinberg?"

"Boy, you are never going to believe what just happened to me and your kids."

It turned out the bats were hiding behind the mats covering the climbing wall, hiding in the hand holds. They were getting into the building through a crack in the wall above our outdoor stairwell. In subsequent years I found a few more, but they were dead behind the mats. It appeared they were unable to leave to get food because the crack was sealed.

13. Bright Idea

Robin Ladd
Retired High School Math Teacher
Seminole and St. Petersburg, Florida
I Love Math!

I taught high school math in an International Baccalaureate program at St. Petersburg High School in St Petersburg, Florida. It is an old school, built in the 1920s. I had a reputation for always being prepared for anything. For example, since we lived in Florida, I had backup plans for hurricanes, so that even if school was cancelled, we could still meet elsewhere, or at least know what to study so that we didn't get behind in preparing for the Advanced Placement or International Baccalaureate tests that occurred at the end of the school year. I also stored popsicles in the teachers' refrigerator and large fans in a closet so if the air conditioning went out, nothing could stop math from happening that day.

So, when I arrived one morning before sunrise to complete darkness, I had to pause. How the heck was I going to make today work? The sun didn't rise till sometime in second period. How were kids going to see to even get to class? The other teachers and administrators who also arrived early were walking around using their cell phones for light. The proper folks had been called to see about fixing the situation, and we were told it could be a few hours before electricity and lights would be restored. I looked toward my classroom area, which was in a corner of the school. It was pitch black. I was wondering how in the world I was going to make this work, and at about the same time, my administrator said to me, "I'm surprised you aren't prepared for this event!" It sparked an idea.

My brother Kevin, who always makes Christmas extra special with cool gifts no one else would ever find, had given me a bowler hat with a light bulb perched on top. I used it in my classroom when students had an especially "bright idea" and it had an incredibly bright light. I used my hands to feel my way to my dark classroom, and then to the spot in the room where I knew the hat was stored. As I turned on the light in the hat, it immediately lightened the room enough to see everything.

About that time, students started arriving at school. I stood at the end of the hall, illuminating the corridor so all students could find their way to their lockers and to their classrooms. It was an unusual start to the day, but we could all see to get the math done, which is all that really mattered, right?

14: What Were You Doing in My Underwear Drawer?

Keith Kremer
Chief Academic Officer
Washington County Public Schools
Plymouth, North Carolina

I was the principal of a large middle school. One of my students was found with a bag of marijuana in his possession. The student would not share with me or with our school resource officer where he got the marijuana or what he planned to do with it.

He was a good student. We called the parents to school. The dad asked the student, "Where would you get something like that from?"

The student clearly did not want to answer. Finally, after relentless prodding by the father, the student said, "From your underwear drawer, Dad."

Dad then asked, "What were you doing in my underwear drawer?" (Using language just a *bit* more impolite.)

It was not a good day for that dad! Oops!

15. Who Let the Goats Out?—Keith Kremer

I was the principal of a small rural high school in North Carolina. Students drove their tractors to school and parked them in the school parking lot. Our school was surrounded by farms. Both of my children were also students at my school. One day, goats got out of their pen and invaded my campus. They were goats from one of my student's farm.

I got on the loudspeaker and sang the song "Who Let the Goats Out?" ("Who Let the Dogs Out?") and called the student to the office.

My children immediately joined me in the office and said in unison, "Never do anything like that again!" I apparently embarrassed them.

16: Skip—Keith Kremer

Skip was a student in my classroom during my first full year of teaching. His twin sister was also in my class, and she was as sweet as a student could be.

Skip was a terror. I worked very hard trying every strategy possible to keep Skip focused. He continued to disrupt the learning of others within my classroom. Finally, while playing "Skip to My Lou" with my children, I was struck with a solution. I took my children's Fisher Price cassette player and the cassette tape with "Skip to my Lou" with me to school.

From that day forward, when I sensed Skip was about to *lose it*, I began playing our song, and the entire class skipped and sang. We lost a little instructional time skipping and singing, but we had a great time doing it plus my negative interactions with Skip went away. In retrospect, Skip probably needed that opportunity to move.

17: Funny and Heartwarming Too—Keith Kremer

I began teaching seventh grade mathematics after graduating from college. I was hired in early May, replacing a teacher who went out on sick leave. One of my students, who I'll call Jacob, had lost his father that same month.

The following school year I looped up with my students, becoming an eighth grade mathematics teacher. Jacob was a student in one of my classes. I remember him coming to class early, staying late, and joining me for my Saturday academies, but I thought that he simply shared my love of mathematics.

Four years later, I was serving as the principal of my first high school. Jacob personally delivered an invitation to his graduation. The graduation at my high school was scheduled for the same day, so I was sure it would be impossible for me to attend.

Then a number of people began visiting me, explaining how important it was for me to be at Jacob's graduation—the senior class advisor, the principal, and Jacob's mom. Then our superintendent came to me and assured me that he had made arrangements to cover my pre-graduation responsibilities for my school.

Graduation was on the football field. This was the feeder school for the middle school where I had taught mathematics for five years before moving into administration. I knew everyone.

Jacob was the valedictorian of his graduating class. During his speech, he shared how his father had passed away the year I became his teacher and how important I had become in his life. He then led, with the assistance of a number of my other former students, the entire audience in a song and dance I used for changing percentages to decimals. It went like this—"Percent to a decimal—two to the left!" (Then everyone jumps two steps to the left.) … "Percent to a decimal, two to the left!" (Two more steps to the left.) … "Percent to a decimal, two to the left!" (Two more steps.) … "And that's the way we do it!"

News cameras and the entire crowd looked up at me, tears rolling down my face. I was a mess.

As a teacher, one rarely knows the impact that we have on individual students. In this case, the student went out of his way to make sure I knew. The moment for me was priceless and will stay with me forever.

18. Technology—Oh My!

Carol J. Baillie
Teacher for 52 years
Bismarck, ND

Having grown up in a rural farming community in the 1940s, I was not at all familiar with technology. We had a battery operated radio, kerosene lamps, limited electricity via a wind charger, outdoor outhouse, a well for water, coal furnace, and gas appliances. About 1947, Rural Electric (REA) provided electricity for most farms in North Dakota. In the next few years, we also had indoor plumbing, telephones, and television. A sheet of blue, red, and green cellophane on the TV screen provided us with color.

Our school supplies consisted of a Big Chief tablet, pencil, and a box of eight crayons. We had to use carbon paper to copy anything. Much work was done on blackboards. When we got to high school, typing classes were offered through correspondence, with no supervision, thus little motivation.

Fortunately in college, I had to write very few papers. On one paper, I apologized for my typing skills. I got a good grade on content, but the instructor added the comment, "You're right, your typing is lousy."

During my early teaching years, much work was done on the board, and later, copying was done on a ditto machine. Teachers were often identified as "teachers" by the blue on their hands. I was able to keep up throughout the years with the help of other teachers, students, and relatives. I even set up a classroom web page with the help of my daughter, but I never felt very techy.

I retired in 2011 and started to substitute in the Bismarck schools. One of my first jobs was at the Career Academy. My husband was leery about me subbing in a technology class, but I decided to give it a try.

The students were producing ads for various products. One student was doing an ad for a soap product, complete with dialogue, animated graphics, music, and bubbles floating up in the background. As I watched in awe, I remarked, "You know, when I was your age, we would have never dreamt of this."

He looked at me with equal amazement and asked, "You mean you didn't have bubbles?"

19: What about the Remainder?—Carol J. Baillie

My brothers and I attended a one room country school with one teacher for the first eight grades. My younger brother, Roger, was having trouble with long division. As the teacher was helping him at the blackboard, a younger student, Karen, said she could do the problem. She went to the board and did it all correctly, except rather than writing "R" for remainder, she wrote a "K". As my brother's name was Roger, her understanding was that you write your initial for the remainder.

20: Roly-Poly—Carol J. Baillie

While student teaching, I was very, very pregnant. It was July and baby was due in August. While explaining to the class that the word *roly-poly* means very round like a ball, one student asked, "Like you, Mrs. Baillie?"

21: The Donut Tree

Kristin Small
Elementary School Assistant Principal
Raleigh, NC

I was a second grade teacher. It was March 31, and we were studying plants in science. We grew a variety of flowers and vegetables from seeds.

I showed pictures of donut trees to my students. The students were excited to grow their own tree. Each student was provided a small paper cup. They partially filled their cups with soil. Each student was then provided a donut seed (a Cheerio). They carefully pushed their finger into the center of their cup and covered their seed with soil.

Later that day they went out for lunch and recess. During that time, our teaching assistant pushed small plants into each student's cup—with a stem strong enough to support a *small donut*. When the students returned to school the next morning, they were thrilled to find small chocolate donuts on their donut trees. A few of the parents had sewn doubt in our students—but *seeing is believing*.

The students told everyone in the school about their project. Some older students played along while others attempted to set my second graders straight.

Before the end of the day—the April Fools' Day Prank was revealed.

22: Oops!

MIKE GROTTE
45 YEARS SHOP TEACHER
RETIRED
GLENBURN, ND

I was a drivers education instructor in Glenburn, North Dakota. One time I was driving with a pair of 14-year-old girls, and I had them pull over for a rest and a chance to change drivers. We were driving one of the more-than-common maroon family vans that were everywhere. The three of us got out and walked around awhile. When I got back to the van, I found a lady sleeping behind the wheel. I was just about to shake her, when out of the window, I see an irate man running towards us. At the same time I spot our maroon van three parking places down to the left. Oops! I bailed out and lived to tell this story.

23: This is No Blizzard!

MICHAEL L. KREMER
LONGTIME EDUCATOR AND ADMINISTRATOR
LEADER OF THE KREMER PACK

My first year of teaching, I awakened to a snowstorm. I followed my normal routine, arriving at school 90 minutes before the contractual starting time. As a first year teacher, I was focused on the day and the lesson plans. My concentration and focus was on students and learning.

All of a sudden I looked up at the clock, and it was 15 minutes after the time all teachers should have been in the building! I panicked, and my first thought was I missed a district wide staff development session. After calming down, I called the building principal who informed me school had been canceled due to the snowstorm. I didn't think this snowstorm was too bad at all. It certainly wouldn't have resulted in school being canceled when I was growing up in North Dakota. My definition of a snowstorm and a day without students in school was modified immediately.

24: Arly's Little Trick—Michael L. Kremer

My first year as a principal was in a rural community, and the second week of school, I receive a call from a community member saying, "The Richau horse is out of the pasture."

My secretary was a community member, and she had been secretary at the elementary school for 25 years. So I placed the call on hold and asked her what the message meant. She told me, "Community members let us know when the horse is loose walking around the community, worried someone might either hit or steal it." She added, "Sixth grader Arly Richau left the pasture gate open often so the past principal would let him go home to put the horse back in the fence.

Almost always, Arly didn't return to school."

So, as a rookie, I decided I knew how to fix that problem. I drove to the area the horse purportedly was located, sweet talked the horse, wrapped my belt around his neck gently, walked it to the pasture, closed the gate, and looked around, truly believing I was on *Candid Camera*.

Over the next two years Arly only let the horse out once, and I did not let him leave the school. Instead, I called the parents who said they would take care of it. Arly did not try his little trick again.

25: Paper Bag on the Desk

KAREN SMINK
TEACHER FOR 25 YEARS, 3RD GENERATION TEACHER
MERRITT ISLAND, FLORIDA
MIAMI DOLPHINS ROCK - SOMETIMES

I've been searching for a story my fourth grade students wrote about 10 years ago. The prompt was, "On my desk is a paper bag. Watch it carefully—there is something inside! During the week, I will give you hints about what is inside, then, on Friday, we will all write a story about the contents of the bag."

So, occasionally during the week, I would pick up the bag, open it just a bit, talk to the contents, feed it lettuce, and scold it for trying to escape!

Finally, Friday arrived. My 22 fourth graders wrote like crazy! It was the quietest hour ever in a fourth grade classroom! Just before I asked volunteers to read their masterpieces, I talked to the bag one more time. I asked the contents to please be patient. The time had come to meet the kids.

After much anticipation, I gently lifted the bag from my desk, s-l-o-w-l-y opened the bag, reached in, and sweetly scooped up the cutest, tiniest, stuffed bunny ever! (That's why I had dropped lettuce in the bag.) The class went wild! There were *oohs* and *ahs* and so much laughter. They got such a kick out of my little bunny that they couldn't even read their own stories! Every time they tried to read about their ideas of the contents, they would melt into puddles of giggles! One girl even fell to the floor, holding her writing in one hand and her sore-from-laughing-too-much belly in her other hand. It was the funnest, funniest writing day ever!

26: Lesson FAIL—Karen Smink

While taking teaching classes at Rollins College in Florida, there came the day when we were to present a science lesson. One of my longtime college friends presented a lesson on *How Mealworms do something*. (This class was over 30 years ago. The title of the lesson is not nearly as important as what happened next.) My friend brought in small containers of mealworms, one container for each group of three or four future teacher students.

At some point during the lesson, the professor decided to teach us a different lesson. He picked up one of the worms and tossed it across the room, hitting my friend right in the face! The class was stunned! Oh, but it didn't stop there! Mr. Somebody decided that everyone needed a lesson in getting hit in the face with the mealworms—not stopping until one of us screeched, "ENOUGH!"

Needless to say, we didn't think it was nearly as funny as he did. When all of us regained our composure, he explained that he was giving us a lesson on how to handle unruly students. HA! Lesson fail, Mr. Teacher! I don't remember seeing him around campus much after that lesson.

27: I told Jeff—*Anonymous Contributor*

Many kindergarten teachers have children in their classrooms that often need help understanding what sort of information the teacher needs to know throughout the school day. Teachers with students who feel compelled to inform the teacher about every classmate's whereabouts and activities throughout the day often develop strategies to help minimize the disruptions. Some teachers have the students write them a note, or they may have a special stuffed animal in the room for students to relay their concerns.

The year this story happened, my class theme was

NASCAR. Jeff Gordon was still racing and was my favorite driver. I had a life-size cutout of Jeff Gordon in my classroom. I talked to my class about the things I needed to know and what I did *not* need to know. For example, I do not need to know Johnny stepped out of line, but I do need to know if he is hitting someone. Our life-size *cutout Jeff* was the "tattletale" guy in our classroom. If it was not something the teacher needed to know, they were to tell Jeff.

I got a call from a parent one afternoon who said her daughter was hit by another student on the playground. The parent asked her daughter if she told her teacher what happened, and the girl responded, "No, I told Jeff." The parents were a little confused on who "Jeff" was, but luckily, they were fellow NASCAR fans and figured it out based on my classroom theme that year. Needless to say, we had another discussion about what information I needed to know and what things "Jeff" needs to know.

28: A Stinky Story

LEE RUSSELL BROWN, GRANDMOTHER
LICENSED PROFESSIONAL COUNSELOR
COLUMBIA, TENNESSEE
NURTURE THE CHILDREN!

Jimmy Jones was an animal skinner from age five. Squirrel, raccoon, mink, rabbit and skunk lived in fear on his father's farm on Snow Creek Road in Santa Fe, Tennessee. The going rate per skin was about ten dollars and little Jimmy saved his money carefully.

After a profitable year, he was advised by his father, "Jimmy, you need to go in town to the bank and get a Social Security card." So the youngster entered First Farmers and Merchants Bank, told them his name was *Jimmy Jones*. (Even after serving 30 years in the U.S. Navy, his Social

Security card still reads *Jimmy Jones*.)

Rescuing frozen baby lambs at 4:00 a.m. on winter mornings was routine to the nine-year-old. But the highlight of his skinning days was yet to come. After arriving at his elementary school, Jimmy spotted a perfectly-marked dead skunk in the school parking lot. He could see dollar signs as clear *as the wide white stripe down the unique animal's back.*

It was the most beautiful skunk he had ever seen! Sitting through arithmetic class was hard, but sitting, period, was agony! His worried thoughts were: *Would someone steal it? ... Would a car run over it?"*

Until recess, he restrained his anxious excitement. When it was time for recess, he quickly rushed from the third grade classroom, sneaked toward the parking lot where—Alas! The prize lay undisturbed.

Whew! Concealing the limp treasure under his shirt, he carried the skunk into the boys' bathroom, took his knife out of his jean pocket, and proceeded to skin the fragrant animal in the sink.

As perfume began to permeate the halls, teachers and students began to wonder, "What is THAT smell?"

With windows thrown open, fans turned on, and noses pinched, everyone began to gag. School pandemonium! Fortunately or rather, unfortunately, a teacher in the school, Jimmy's mother, no less, rushed him home to hopefully smother the smell and bathe the lad in hot soapy water.

The school stayed stinky for days.

29: BUG BUSTERS IN SOUTH CAROLINA—
ANONYMOUS CONTRIBUTOR

I teach kindergarten in South Carolina. Unfortunately, we sometimes have issues with bugs in our classrooms. One day, I noticed several Palmetto bugs going in and out of the floor drains of the class bathroom. Palmetto bugs are a nice name for the giant cockroaches that are native to coastal South Carolina, who mostly live outside, but occasionally try to *move indoors* during weather extremes.

After seeing several Palmetto bugs near a floor drain in the bathroom, I reported the problem to the district. Unfortunately, they decided to pour liquid bug killer down the drains in my classroom while we were at lunch.

When we returned to our classroom after lunch hour, it looked like a horror movie coming to life. Roaches were everywhere—crawling out of the drains, up the walls, across the floor. EEEEEEEKKKK!

I tried to stay calm and immediately turned my class around and told them we would use the restrooms down the hall. In the meantime, my brave assistant and a custodian went into the classroom to battle the bugs. My assistant was seen smacking the bugs with her shoe, and the custodian looked like one of the *Ghost Busters* with a vacuum canister strapped to his back and his hose sucking up the bugs.

It was truly a nightmare come to life. Not really a funny story to me at the time, because I am afraid of bugs, but I look back and laugh when remembering my assistant and our wonderful custodian battling the bugs!

30: Riding the Struggle Bus

Jennifer Hayes
Wife, Mom and Teacher of tiny humans!
Minot, ND

I once made the mistake of expressing my thoughts aloud and told my kiddos that we were *riding the struggle bus*. The rest of the day I had a kid tell me that *he* wanted to ride the struggle bus. He was very upset with me when I informed him that he couldn't ride the struggle bus, and he would have to ride home with his mom. As I was walking him down the hall to be picked up at the end of the day, he had his head hanging down and looked very sad. Someone stopped and asked him why he was so sad and he said, "I just want to ride the struggle bus."

FUNNY STORIES

31: YOU NEVER WANT THAT TAKEN OUT!

DARLENE PAULSON
WIFE, MOTHER, GRANDMOTHER
RETIRED TEACHER
VERGAS, MINNESOTA

While teaching second grade, Ryan was holding his side, frowning, and he came up to me. I asked, "Are you feeling okay?"

He answered, "Yeah, but my mom went to the hospital last night and had her independence tooken out."

32: Aunt Dolores Had to Sit under the Teacher's Desk

Dolores Kremer Wells
Wife, Mother, Teacher
Cook, Tennis Player, Golfer (I even got a hole in one!)
Gardener, Bowler, Animal lover
Being a grandma and great-grandma is the best!

Aunt Dolores remembers having to sit under the teacher's desk when she was talking to a boy at Linton Elementary School, but she didn't mind. The boy she had been talking to had to sit under the desk with her—and Dolores *kind* of liked him.

33: Tissue Flowers

JOAN NELSON AUCH -BHS '69
RETIRED RN, HENDERSONVILLE, TN
GRAMMY IS MY FAVORITE ROLE
BLESSED TO BE RAISED IN BISMARCK

When I was a third grader at Will-Moore Elementary School in Bismarck in 1959, I had Miss Beth Fuxa as my teacher. Sadly, during the winter she became ill, and after a hospital stay, she was home recovering for six weeks.

We missed her so much and made a *Welcome Back* banner when she came back to school. The whole class helped create it. A friend and I volunteered to create tissue flowers by folding multiple tissues together in a fan-like fashion.

Well, both of my folks worked full-time to provide for us, and I now know what a sacrifice of love that large container of Chanel #5 was for my dad to give mom that Christmas just prior to Miss Fuxa's illness. But I was a third grader home alone, and my friend and I loved my teacher so much. I loved the smell of that perfume and decided that it would be the perfect finishing touch on those 10 paper flowers. So, I just sprayed away till they were pretty saturated with that lovely fragrance. When I was done, there was no more spray!

Amazingly, my parents didn't scold me. I think they were so pleased with where my heart was that all was forgiven. Now that I'm grown and still love that perfume, I realize that those flowers were a gift of love not only from me, but also from my parents!

34. Line Up for Your Shots

CARLENE FITTERER
ELEMENTARY TEACHER
BISMARCK, NORTH DAKOTA
LOVES BOOKS!

It was April Fools' Day. When my third graders came inside following the last recess of the day, I told them we needed to get drinks quickly before lining up to go down to the lunchroom for their shots. Some voiced concerns, but I assured them their parents were okay with this. After the drinks, we lined up to go downstairs. After arriving there, all the children saw were empty lunchroom tables. I informed them the nurses were in the kitchen area. After squeezing inside, I said, "April Fools!"

Some responded, "Miss Fitterer!" in total surprise. Others showed their complete relief.

April Fools' Day—mission accomplished! I was not known to pull tricks on my students, but this one time, I did it.

35. How Long?—Carlene Fitterer

I taught third grade at Pioneer Elementary School in Bismarck for many years with Winnie Hoersch, and she told me this story.

Benny had been misbehaving almost daily. Winnie called him out of her classroom, into the hallway.

She asked him, "Just how long do you think I'm going to put up with this behavior?"

Benny opened his eyes, blinked his long brown eyelashes, and said, "Another *day*?"

Peering over her half-lens glasses, she answered, "Not another **minute**!"

36: I Was Buying Drugs—anonymous contributor

After an evening college class that I was teaching had just ended, a student came up to me and said matter-of-factly, "Sorry I missed class, but I was out buying drugs."

The student was working as an undercover agent for the State Bureau of Criminal Investigation.

37. Hup, Two, Three, Four—about (losing) face!

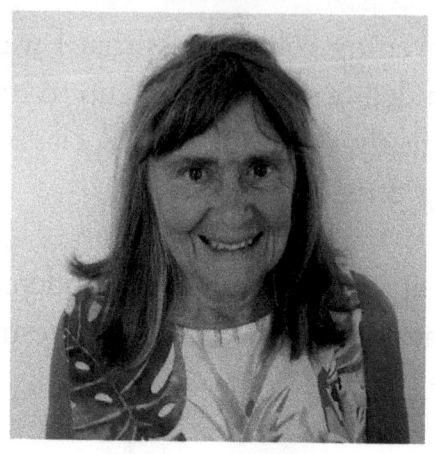

Carolyn King
Retired Natural Foods Sales Rep
Grand Rapids, Minnesota
Happiest when I'm in the water!

It is the fall of 1962 and the Central Football team is on a roll. Co-Captains Ron Bergh and Dick Koons are leading the team to one victory after another. But the big game, the major rivalry, is yet to be played. The Fargo contest is scheduled for mid-October and that's the one we really want to win.

But hold on, this article isn't about the football team, it's really about the band. Under the direction of Bill Pond, we had been performing halftime shows at the home games. For the game with

Fargo, Mr. Pond wanted to do something special so he chose a select group of us to be a drill team. He wrote out the routine so we could learn all the moves, and we spent the week before the game practicing at the Valley Junior High football field. By the day of the game we were a fine-tuned machine.

It was a crisp autumn evening under the lights of the UND football stadium. There was a big crowd, and the football cheerleaders—Charlotte Ensrud, Kristi Bethke, Patty Gorman, Wendy Kielty, Pam Ollman and Doreen Kristjanson—had the fans in a frenzy. The game was going great but now it was halftime and our drill team was pumped-up and ready to perform. We proudly marched onto the field in our maroon and gray uniforms with Mr. Pond *calling the plays*. Everything was going as planned until Mr. Pond had a lapse in memory and called out the wrong move. In that split second, each of us made a decision—half of us did what he said and the other half did what we were supposed to do. The result was a jumbled mess of everyone bumping into each other on the 50-yard line.

We froze not knowing what to do next, and all we could hear was the uproar of laughter coming from the crowd in the stands. I noticed Tom Micklin frantically lugging his tuba, trying to figure out where he was supposed to go. Then he caught my eye and, we, too, broke out into laughter. It was a great moment! I can't remember how or if we recovered and if we ever finished the routine, but to this day, when I recall it, I still break out into a big grin. It was one of the most humiliating and hilarious moments in my life!

The band may have goofed but the football team came through: Central beat Fargo 13 to nothing!

38. Stolen Lunch

Mary Baird
Retired Teacher
Bismarck, ND

I taught junior high and high school English for 37 years. Here is my favorite story. A very sweet female janitor at our school complained to me that her lunch was being stolen every day. She said it had to be the head janitor, who was a male, because they were the only two who had access to the janitor's closet besides the superintendent, and she highly doubted it was he.

After several days, I told her I had a plan to help. I went to the local grocery store and bought a brownie mix, then walked across the street to the local drug store and bought a package of chocolate Ex-Lax. I made the brownies, slathered on the melted Ex-Lax, cut two big pieces, wrapped them up, and had them waiting for her in my classroom when she got to work the next morning. She took them and put them with her lunch that day.

She had confided in the social studies teacher, also, so I felt I should tell him about our nefarious plan. Well, sure enough, her lunch was gone when she went to retrieve it, including the *special* brownies.

This male janitor also drove the school bus for out of town basketball games, and we had one that night. Interestingly, the social studies teacher was the students' chaperone. The next morning over coffee, the social studies teacher told me that the head janitor/bus driver was going up and down the bleachers all through the game! He talked to the janitor and asked if he was okay. The janitor said he just had not been feeling well all night—tummy troubles.

The kicker is, my social studies friend told him, "Gee, I don't know. Maybe you picked up something."

From that day on, her lunch was never stolen again. Sometimes that's the only way people learn!

39: Tying Shoes

Carlene Bahm
Teacher, Rancher's Wife
Mother, Grandmother, Quilter,
Mandan, North Dakota

I was teaching in a multi-graded classroom. I was down on my knees tying a little boy's shoes when I said, "Tommy, you need to learn to tie your shoe."

He patted me on the head and said, "Don't worry, Mrs. Bahm. My dad can't tie his shoes either."

40: I Need an Ambulance—*Anonymous Contributor*

One morning as we were taking our group of special needs kids to school, one of the little ones showed us a small *booboo* on his forearm. He was very concerned about the small injury. We gave him sympathy, and upon arriving at school and unloading our kids, this little guy stepped off the bus into the waiting arms of a school aide, pointed to the sore place, and loudly said: "I need an AMBULANCE!"

The school aide couldn't help herself. She burst out laughing and my bus driver and I were laughing also.

41: That Jump Rope Didn't Stop Us

Ed Trejo
Korean and Vietnam War Veteran
Silver Star and Distinguished Flying Cross Recipient
Goose Creek, South Carolina

I was in the first grade and two of my friends and I were misbehaving one day—so our teacher eventually tied us up together with a jump rope. When the rest of the kids in our class went out for recess, we got loose and went out for recess ourselves. The teacher wasn't too happy when she found out about it. She sent us to the principal.

42. The Pretty Dress

Norene Sandberg
Married 48 years
Five Grandkids
Life is Good!

As a first grader our daughter got a speaking part for her classroom's Thanksgiving play. I chose a pretty dress for her to wear for the program. She put up quite a fuss that morning having to wear the dress stating, "But Mom, I won't get to play on the monkey bars during recess if I wear a dress."

My suggestion was for her to wear her jeans under her dress during recess time. Problem solved, right? Well, later that day as I attended the Thanksgiving play, there she was, front and center, ready for the program with her pretty little dress neatly tucked in to her jeans!

43. Watch Out for Those Brainstorms!

Peggy Kopp
Taught special needs for six years
Taught fifth grade for 27 years
Library media specialist for two years
Bismarck Public Schools

My fifth grade classroom was an active group with many special needs students integrated into the class. They were getting ready to start a new project so I put the students into small groups so they could work together as a team. The first day I told the groups to brainstorm ideas on what they wanted to do.

After a few minutes, a special needs student came up to me looking very puzzled and worried. She wanted to know if *brainstorming* meant that thunder and lightning would go off in her head. I quickly assured her that it meant for the students to share ideas that they had in mind.

She was so relieved and happily joined her group. I wonder what other things I had said in the past that I should have clarified.

44. Our Kid Will Pay for the Gas

Sue Triska
Pioneer Elementary Teacher, Bismarck, 38 years
Retired and took up golfing
Loves being a Grandma!

I had a parent-teacher conference where the parents told me if their son ever forgot something and wanted them to bring it to school—he would have to pay for the gas! It worked. Their son very seldom had to call home!

45. How can you beat a steak?—Sue Triska

Two sixth grade boys *supposedly* went home for lunch, but instead, they ran up to North American Steak Buffet to eat. Our noon break was only 40 minutes long. It was quite a distance from the school to the steak buffet, and the boys had to cross busy Highway 83 to get there. Their plan was working out great—except one of our teacher aides saw them cross the highway as she was returning to school. The boys didn't make it back before the bell rang so they were tardy!

Our aide came to see me and check on the boys. When I questioned the sixth grade boy in my class, he said, "I was *really* hungry and a steak sounded good!"

46. Who Let the Dogs Out?—Sue Triska

It was the day after Halloween in 2000. My students were in an excited mood. Too much candy the night before, I'm sure! But we had also received some new desks. My kids were excited to move into them and have a new seating arrangement.

That afternoon the tornado warning sirens went off. Several tornados were sighted in our area, and we needed to exit our classroom and shelter in place in the girls' bathroom—much to the dismay of the boys. I assured them it was the best place to go and probably cleaner than their bathroom.

We were in there all afternoon. Some of the younger siblings were scared and started crying so they were brought to the girls' bathroom to be with their older siblings. I told my class to sing songs to them—anything to get their minds off the tornado.

As I was going between the hallway and the bathroom, supervising, I could hear singing! I heard "Happy Birthday" and then "Who Let the Dogs Out?"—my favorite song at the time. The crying stopped, and it was followed by lots of laughter!

47. Clearing the Lunch Table!

Wayne Triska
Teacher for Students with Vision Impairments
and
Mobility Instructor for 37 years
Retired and busy
Bismarck, North Dakota

I had a student who was blind with prosthetic eyes attending all regular classes in a large middle school. During lunch other students begin asking questions about his eyes. In an effort to present the most information, the student popped out his prosthetic eyes and so grossed out the other students that the lunch table totally cleared. The principal was not impressed, and as a result the student received three days in-school suspension.

48. I swallowed my eye!—Wayne Triska

There was a blind student with prosthetic eyes attending a preschool program at the age of three who swallowed one of his prosthetic eyes. It caused quite a stir at school. The parents waited for the eye to pass and it didn't. The doctor eventually had the student swallow some wetted cotton and it passed. The eye was washed up, put back in, and good to go.

49. I can insert that prosthetic eye?—Wayne Triska

A preschool girl who was blind with prosthetic eyes had one eye come out in school. The occupational therapist, who is very energetic and always ready for a learning experience, gathered all the preschool teachers together so the vision teacher could show everyone how to reinsert a prosthetic eye. The anxious vision teacher, who had never seen a prosthetic outside the student's socket, was in a situation. He had witnessed people placing contacts in their eyes so he figured it could not be that much different. So, with all the staff watching, he lifted up the eyelids of the little girl and inserted the prosthetic eye. All was good until the little girl looked up at the staff, and the eye was upside down. The little girl just turned it around and looked great.

50. Right-side up!—Wayne Triska

There was a blind student who was not known to write for very long on his braille writer, but this time, he wrote a story a page and a half long. His classroom teacher dog-eared the two pages together at the top and gave it to the vision teacher for interlining (writing the words above the braille).

The vision teacher tried in vain to decipher the story. The braille did not make sense and was not even words. The vision teacher surmised that the student had just brailled randomly for length to impress the teacher. The vision teacher returned the braille story to the classroom teacher with the bad news that no story was written.

The classroom teacher, in her wisdom, asked if the braille was upside down. It was a pretty decent story when right side up. The classroom teacher, known to play a joke or two, may have dog-eared the story the wrong way on purpose.

Part 2: Funny Stories from Joni Magstadt's Second Grade Class

After teaching 34 years, Joni retired in 2015. Since then, she has been serving on the Kidder County School Board and subbing a lot—which helps Joni get her *kid fix*. Joni's stories come from her last seven years of teaching. Currently, she spends much of her time driving John Deere tractors and being a professional procrastinator.

1. The flies had been relentless this week in our classroom, and after I swatted one on a little guy's desk, he piped up, "One down, a gazillion to go!"

***

2. We take daily movement breaks to "Let's Dance" videos for kids. I enjoy them as much as the class does. One day after one of these videos, one of my boys said, "We should have a disco ball in our room when we dance!"

***

3. To demonstrate how quickly we can get off a topic in second grade, this was a conversation that went on this week:

While doing math on our marker boards—the Commutative Property of Addition to be specific—I swatted two very annoying flies at once that were close together on someone's desk. I made the mistake of saying, "Hey, I got two with one swat!"

Student: "Sometimes I can hit two flies at once, if they are on top of each other."

Another student: "Yeah, you can. I've done that!"

Student: "This summer I saw two dragonflies on top of each other."

Another student: "Yeah, I've seen them riding piggyback too!"

Another student: "Me, too, that's really cool!"

And yet another student: "Me too. I've seen grasshoppers do that."

Another student: "It's like when cows jump on each other's backs."

Student: "Why do they do that?"

The kid with the answer: "They're just playing around."

And back to math we go...

4. Today, following the Homecoming Parade, a second grader told me, "I think I'll give the fireballs I got to my dad. He really likes them."

Me: "Well, that's really nice of you to share your candy!"

Second grader: "I really don't like them all that much anyway!"

***

5. Thursday we had a pep rally for Homecoming Week. Some of the students couldn't remember the pep rallies from the past year so I tried to explain to them what pep rallies were for and some things that might happen at them. When we came back to the classroom, I asked, "So, what do you think?"

Student: "Pepper rallies are lots of fun!"

***

6. Student: "Mrs. Magstadt, do you know the Wild West is where Scheels is?"

Comments like this just come up out of the blue— like right in the middle of math class or as I am dismissing rows for lunch—so I am caught off-guard quite often!

Me: "What!?"

Student: "Yeah, my dad told me and he knows. The Wild West was where Scheels is, you know, that store in Bismarck." *Dads are never wrong.*

"My Dad spent all my mom's Christmas money on a dog. He just had to have a German Shepherd!" *I couldn't wait to tell the Mom what I was told!*

After recess a little girl came up to me to tell me, "At recess my feet and head were sweatin' hot, and the rest of me was freezing!" Touching her forehead, she said, "Here, feel my sweat. It's just juicy!" *Ewww!*

We have had *so* many loose teeth in our class lately and some of the teeth hung on forever, all crooked, hanging by a thread, before they came completely out. When one little guy finally lost his loose tooth, he said to me, "Now that my tooth is gone, I can listen more better."

"Teacher, I'm so buff and strong that I don't cry when I get hurt. My sisters can't even make me cry cuz I'm buffer than they are."

***

7. On shirts the kids are wearing:

"Dear Santa—Yes, I'm naughty, but I'm good at it!"

"Dear Santa—Have I been good enough?"

***

8. Question of the week:

What is the hardest question in the world to answer?

How come I have none of my memory from when I was a baby?
What happened to the *Titanic*?
How many girls are in the world?
How many cats and dogs are in the world?

How was God born?
What happened to the dinosaurs?
How many days are in a year?
How do you say *one* in Spanish?
How many people are in the world cuz I think there's too much to count?
Who was the first person to discover Bigfoot?
How do scientists get so smart?
Who invented the colors?
What is 1,500 + 78,600?
What is 1,000 x 5,000?
What is 1,000 x 1,00000,0000,0000,0000,0000,0000,0000,0000,0000,0000,0000,0000?

On a side note, I recently read about a study that determined that second grade teachers answer an average of 1,700 questions a day! I believe it!

***

9. After changing to the new monthly calendar, I asked the second graders if they could name the two important holidays in November.

First student: "Thanksgiving!"

Second little boy, completely serious: "I know, I know! … Deer Season!"

10. Overheard in the hall:

"I think my leg is broken!"
"No, if it was broken, you'd be crying really hard."
"Well, I *feel* like crying really hard!"

***

11. While getting ready to work on our NWEA tests (Northwest Evaluation Association) Mr. Kallenbach went up to his computer to confirm the tests and one of the kids said, "Mr. K is smart."

Second student: "So is Mrs. Magstadt!"

Third student: "Well, they're teachers! Of course, they're smart!"

I gave the kids granola bars as a treat after finishing up their tests. One little guy piped up, "I sure do like these canoga bars!"

***

12. "Mrs. Magstadt, did you know I'm more awesomer than I was yesterday? I'm funny that way."

13. *What is your mom's favorite thing to do?*

My mom's favorite thing to do is relax.
My mom's favorite thing to do is to drive because she loves to drive and go anywhere.
My mom's favorite thing to do is eat ice.
My mom's favorite thing to do is spend time with me. (*Ahhh*)
My mom's favorite thing to do is driving bus.
My mom's favorite thing to do is to cook.
My mom likes to cuddle with me.
My mom likes to cook.
My mom likes to clean house.
My mom likes to say *I love you*.
My mom likes to stay home and watch TV.
My mom likes taking a nap.
My mom likes to read books.
My mom likes to work on the computer.
My mom likes to spend money on stuff.

***

14. After discussing Veterans Day a student commented, "My uncle is too old to be in the army."

Me: "That's too bad."
Student: "Yeah, he's dead."

15. Student: "Mrs. Magstadt, do you know why I put KFC as my favorite restaurant?"

Me: "Is it because you like chicken?"

Student, with a smile: "No, its cuz I could spell it!"

Reminds me of the time a little girl asked me how to spell MDU.

***

16. We were discussing the word *law* and what it means, and I used the example of the speed limit on the Interstate as one of our laws … or maybe not.

Me: "One of our laws would be that you can't drive over 75 miles an hour on the Interstate."

Student, with utmost confidence: "My mom can, she can drive 80!"

Me: "Hmm, really? Why is that?"

Student: "Cuz the cop told her she could if she wanted to. So she does."

17. Direct quote from a student: "Mrs. Magstadt, I think you're probably gonna really maybe like it a lot!"

***

18. I asked my students to write down three things they would like to do in their lives and here are some of their answers:

Play football and jerk some guys down, be a farmer and chase cattle and ride bulls.

Get a car, be a fireman, and help people.

Go to Disneyland, live in New York, and have a really big party.

Travel across the world, see penguins, and go to the moon.

I want to be a cowgirl, have some toddlers, and be a zookeeper.

Ride in a limo, work at a candy store, and also work at Justice. *That's where all the cute clothes are.*

Be a fireman, get married, get a job, and act like a grown-up.

Live in a mansion, get money, and stay up as late as I want.

***

19. One of our stories this week was about the use of homing pigeons in World War I. Upon seeing the pictures of tanks and soldiers in uniform, one of my students said, "My grandpa and dad were in the army."

Another student responded, "What team were they on?"

***

20. One of my students, absent one day, came back and said, "Do you know why I was gone?"

"Yes, you were sick."

"I was *really* sick! I had a temperature of 99, but this morning it was 91 so I could come to school."

***

21. All the kids had left for the day except for one little guy, who was still getting his gear on and

still talking. "I have a bad headache. It's from all the talking."

My response: "Maybe you shouldn't talk so much then."

"Are you saying I talk a lot? Cuz I don't, it's the other kids."

***

22. From a student: "Did you know that when you put headphones on, no one else can hear you when you talk?"

Hmmm—must just be ME then.

***

23. We had been answering some fun questions about Santa such as:

Why is Santa's suit red? What does Mrs. Claus do to help Santa get ready for Christmas?

So I very innocently asked, "Why do you think Santa is so fat?"

Some responses:

"If he was skinny, he wouldn't fit in his suit."

"Every time he eats all those cookies, he gets a little more chubbier."

***

24. We were discussing synonyms for *sad*. The kids came up with unhappy, gloomy, glum, and blue.

Student: "Blue?"

Me: "Yes, when someone is sad, you can also say they are feeling blue."

Student: "How about *red*, can people feel red?"

Another student: "If they are embarrassed, they turn red so that would be feeling red. Right, Mrs. Magstadt?"

***

25. We watched a couple of videos this week of houses with Christmas lights set to music, which,

if you have ever seen them, are simply amazing. Here are a couple of cute comments that followed the video:

"How can they unplug those lights that fast?"

"I want a house like that!"

"God maybe did that for the kids that live there."

***

26. As I walked by a trio of third grade girls who were talking quietly, I stuck my head in next to theirs and pretended to listen to their conversation. "Look out, Mrs. Magstadt is *earsdropping*!"

***

27. We had some *beautiful* recess days these past couple of weeks with the temperature just perfect for making snowballs and snowmen. One of my little guys came in all excited and said, "There are just tons of snowmans outside!

"SnowMANS?" I said.

He thought awhile and then, with a smile, he said, "I mean snowMEN."

He continued to take his outdoor gear off, and as he turned to another second grader, I heard him say, "Did you see all those snowMANS outside?"

***

28. Interesting comments:

"They were selling free hats."

"I was sweating really fast. I think everybody was."

***

29. On the way out to recess a student stopped by my desk and said, "I used to get in a lot of trouble at my old school."

Me: "Really? You sure are good here. Why do you suppose that is?"

He thought for a while and said, as sincerely as could be, "I think it's cuz you are a good teacher. That makes me good."

And he bopped on out the door, leaving me with a big smile on my face!

30. As part of the 100th day of school this past week, the kids finished some sentence starters for me.
When I am 100 I will...

relax
see my kids
give my farm to my sister
die
give a kiss goodbye
be a grandpa
retire
have grandkids
buy cars
go home
be dead
have a cane
take a nap
want 100 kittens
do a backflip
When I asked, "Why would you do a backflip?" The answer was, "I'll be so happy to be 100!"

***

31. Another one of the sentence starters was: I can't eat 100...

As I was proofreading the responses, I came upon one that said, "I can't eat 100 butt cakes."

To clarify, I asked the student if that was supposed to say butt cakes. He said yes.

"What kind of cake is that?"

He said, "It is a cake that looks like a butt so we call it *butt cake*."

Turns out that when he was little he couldn't pronounce his n's very well so "Bundt cake" became, still is, and probably always will be *butt cake*. Best laugh of the day that day!

***

32. "Mrs. Magstadt, you look like a high schooler today."
"Hey, thanks. Why do you say that?"
"Cuz you have high schooler shoes on!" (sneakers)

***

33. Picture this: Kindergarten, first, and second graders lined up at the door to go in following a recess that was nothing but trouble. I was on

duty. I just finished a talk about the purpose of recess and how it's a privilege and we don't have to have it if kids can't get along. *Blah, blah blah.* I'm sure that's what the kids heard anyway! Let's just say I was slightly crabby.

By my elbow a little guy pulled on my sleeve and said ever so brightly, "I love you, Mrs. Magstadt."

I *had* to smile and I said to him, "I sure do like you a whole lot too, kiddo."

He tips his head to the side, looks at me quizzically and says, "But I said *I love you.*"

Okay, my mistake!

"Yes, I love you too. That's better." *And it is, isn't it!*

***

34. Bathroom door duty: Boys were taking a really long time in the bathroom so I called, "Hey guys! Let's get done in there! What's taking so long anyway?"

Answer as they come out the door: "We're naming the toilets."

"What?"

"We're naming the toilets."

Don't you just wonder sometimes.

***

35. Girls in the bathroom: Four stalls, all girls standing in a line by one stall.

"Girls, what are you doing?"

"We need to go to the bathroom."

"Yes, well, the other stalls are empty."

"We want to use this one."

"Why?"

"It's the best one."

I guess I never knew that.

36. We have a behavior chart in our classroom where each child has a marker that can be moved up (for good) and down (for not-so-good) behavior. One day this week, *nobody* got moved down and they were all really excited about it—including the teacher! One little guy pipes up, "It's like a Thanksgiving miracle!"

I'm so so thankful for kids and the wonderful things they say and do to make me smile! Happy Thanksgiving everyone!

***

37. Here are some comments that you probably won't hear in most second grade classrooms, but you would hear in ours:

"Are you guys calving yet?"
"How many calves do you have?"

"We have more heifers than bull calves, heifers are girls ya know."

"My dad tries to spike 'em if the mom doesn't have milk." *Which leads to an explanation of spiking.*

"Her bag was so big it was dragging on the ground."

"Have you been giving our bull treats?"

"We had a cow with a prolapse."

"We had a cow with one of those too! It looked like a giant strawberry. It was gross."

"My cow had a calf!" *Always a happy announcement!*

"Sometimes my dad has to put his hand in the cow and pull the calf out." *Someone say, "Ewwww!"*

"You have to have bulls to have calves." *No comment.*

I gotta admit—I love this time of year!

***

38. Question of the Week: If you could make one rule that all the people in the world had to follow, what would it be?

Let me be President.
Ice cream for every meal.
My rule would be NO RULES!
Never have homework.
No more smoking allowed anywhere!
No cleaning your room!

Stop all the wars.
Everybody would have to give me a million dollars.
Everybody has to go to Walmart every day! *Yikes*!
Everybody has to get a new kitten every day.
The rule should be, "Listen to other people."
If I could make one rule it would be to follow all the rules.

***

39. Saturday, as I was checking out at Walmart, the last thing I placed on the counter was a pile of 18 bubble wands. The elderly gentleman behind me in line said, "You must have a lot of grandkids!"

I laughed and said, "No grandkids yet, but they are a little Easter treat for a class of second graders!"

He then asked me where I taught and if I had to pay for them myself or if the school paid for things like that. I said, "Oh no, we pay for them, not the school."

When I moved on up to pay, he tapped me on the shoulder and said, "I want to pay for those for you. I know teachers don't make near enough money for all the work they do."

How absolutely nice was that! Well, that guy got a hug and I am still smiling!

***

40. Our class was discussing the meaning of the word *antique*. I commented that antiques are things 40 years old or older. One young man scrunched up his face in thought and said, "Well, *you* would be an antique, Mrs. Magstadt!"

Me: "I don't think people can be antiques."

Student: "How about this school? How old is this school?"

Me: "How old do you think it is?"

Student: "It's gotta be 60 like you cuz you've been teaching forever!"

***

41. One morning, before school, one little guy came back from the bathroom and said, "Mrs.

Magstadt, look at my hair! It growed a lot overnight!"

Me: "It was about that long yesterday, I think."
Little guy: "Oh no, it's like one day you wake up, and all of a sudden you need a haircut!"

***

42. While watching a Christmas movie on Tuesday afternoon, I asked one little fella to please stop talking so the rest of us could hear. To which he replied, "I wasn't talking. I was just answering Tommy because he was talking to *me*!"

Gotta love second grade reasoning!

***

43. Random comments that I loved this week:

"Mrs. Magstadt, what are mouse guts?"

Student who has had loose teeth for months: "There is just too much going on in my mouth!"

Conversation among students about whether or not Santa Claus is real or not. "Well, if you believe in Santa, he will come to your house, so you better start believing right now!"

***

44. Written responses to the question—*What is one thing your teacher should get from Santa Claus?*

a new Jon Deer tractor
a chalkboard because she doesnt have one
a tv to watch
a Jonn Deer tracktor
a fox
a new dog because she loves dogs
a John deer tracker because she loves them
a John deer tracktor
a coffee maker because she LOVES coffee
a pony to ride
coffee because she loves it
a tutu so she can do ballet
a tractor because she is nice
a green tractor, it HAS to be green

***

45. Written responses to the question—*Santa has three new reindeer, what would you name them?*

Jack, Sky, and Mike

Star, Roger, and Jumpy
Diamond, Jane, and Sara
Flicka, Blaze, and Patricky
Skips, Flutterfly, and Foxy
Trey, Abby, and Batman
Mrs. Claus, Santa Claus, and Jerome
Snow White, Beautiful, and Bella
Lilly, Ice Cream, and Jolly
Gun, Zoo, and Sun
Dusty, Sam, and Scruffy
Chocolate, Peanut Butter, and Crazy
Captain, Chaser, Vixo
Bri, Rose, and Edward
Vic, Val, and Dale
Norman1, Norman 2, and Norman 3

***

46. Some more great T-shirts around school:

Famous for my Smile
#1 Rule - Si Did It (referring to Duck Dynasty, I think!)
Don't you DARE read my shirt!
Trouble Can't find Me in Camo
Sweet, Sassy, Awesome
What's Shakin Bacon?

47. After asking one of the kids a question, his answer was, "Yes, Mrs. Magstadt, John Deere Queen."

***

48. One of my students wanted me to check out what he had been doing on a math website on the computer. When I saw his work, I said, "Wow! That looks hard!"

He replied, "I figured I should do something hard to impress you!"

***

49. Second graders have to learn many really hard, long words—how to pronounce them and what they mean. Some of the hardest for them to say are *quadrilateral* (quallitaterall), *declarative* (claralive), *interrogative* (interrgate) *exclamatory*, (exatory) not to be confused with *exclamation*, just to name a few. (*I included how I remember some of them being pronounced just this week.*)

Well, one day we watched a video on the commutative property of addition, and it turns out that I have been pronouncing *commutative* incorrectly. After the video, I told the kids, "Well,

I guess I better start saying that word correctly!"

One little guy, bless his heart said, "*You're* probably right. That guy on the video is wrong!"

***

50. So if you are not too excited about the snow, I can send you a roomful of second graders who are really looking forward to it. They can't wait! When I asked them about why they like snow so much, one of the comments was, "Well, we haven't had any for a really long time!"

***

51. Newsflash! Report of really bad words that were said at the dinner table. Get ready ... NUT and FAT. Luckily, not on the same day or by the same person. *Whew!*

***

52. Students were working on vocabulary, filling in missing words, when they came to a sentence that said _____chip cookies. I said, "Oh, this is something I really like!"

Of course they knew it was *chocolate*! The next comment was, "Mrs. Magstadt, you really like chocolate, but you don't like it better than *us*. You don't like anything better than us!"

***

53. The preschool, kindergarten, and first grade classes walk down the hallway by our room on their way out to recesses each day. One day there was a knock on my door. I opened it, and a little one on his way to recess said, "Teacher, can you help me with my gloves?"

"Sure, kiddo."

He giggled and said, "I love it when you call me kiddo!"

***

54. Another day a little Kinder was coming in from recess, making some really loud noises, so I walked close to her and told her she shouldn't be yelling when she walked down the hall. That didn't faze her so I leaned down close and whispered, "You need to be quiet when you walk down this hall."

She looked at me with a puzzled expression and whispered back, "I don't know quiet."

***

55. We read a book about Martin Luther King, Jr. on Friday. The second graders really took it seriously. When they came in from recess, a little gal said, "We had a great recess, everybody got along. Just like Martin Luther King wants us to."

***

56. There's dog tired, dead tired, and bone tired, but there's nothing like teacher tired *on a Friday*!

***

57. My class was adding three-digit numbers with regrouping one day, as well as practicing writing plurals for the labels. The sum of one problem was 1,032. They then had to write the plural of the word *calf* for a label. Later, as we walked to lunch, one of my farm kids said, "You know Mrs. Magstadt, if you had 1,032 calves, you'd have 1,032 cows too. I don't think you'd have that many calves though, 'cause you'd probably lose a few, like maybe four?"

"If you had that many cows, you would be lucky to lose only four!" I answered.

After thinking a bit he said, "Yeah, if you were unlucky you might lose five!"

Love that optimism!

***

58. We were tearing some pages out of the front of a math workbook that we wouldn't need anymore, and one little guy asked if he could keep them. He said, "That way I can be *occupied* at home when I have nothing to do."

***

59. Learning to write plurals is always fun!

Plural of:

Child ... kids
Moose ... mooses
Mouse ... mices
Calf ... calfs or calfes

Woman ... three womans
Man ... two mans

***

60. As the first and second graders were lining up after the recess bell to come in, I complimented one of the first graders on how quickly and quietly he lined up. Later he told his teacher, "I impressed Mrs. Magstadt, and she's not easy to impress!"

He's right!

***

61. In honor of Martin Luther King Jr. Day on Monday, I want to share this story from a few years back:

My class and I were walking down the sidewalk, two by two, on a field trip to the fire station. Next to me at the front of the line were a little Hispanic boy and an African American boy, holding hands and chatting away. The little African American boy was excited as he said, "Mrs. Magstadt, did you know me and him are twins?"

Surprised at hearing this I said, "Really? Well,

you both have beautiful black hair for one thing."

He responded, all smiles, and said, "Yup! And I'm black and he's *almost* black!"

***

62. We are on Christmas break I will share one of my favorite stories from way back.

I had a little guy who lived close to the school, and he was always the first one to arrive. One day he popped in, all smiles as usual, started talking (as usual), and unzipped his jacket. Just like that, he looked down, stopped talking for a second, zipped his jacket back up really fast and said, "I gotta go home."

"Why?"

As he headed out the door he said, "I forgot my shirt."

***

63. Desk scrubbing day was always lots of fun, especially for those second graders who always

seemed to get more glue on their desks than they did on the actual art project. The desks were sprayed with cleaner and the kids were using scrubbies, working away, when I told one little boy, "You better use some elbow grease on your desk."

Next time I turned around he was, *literally*, scrubbing his desk with his elbow—as serious as he could be.

***

64. Second graders are always super-excited to begin learning cursive handwriting. So one day a second grader asked, "When are we going to start cursive?"

"Oh, we won't start that till January 1," I said.

A little girl with a very worried look on her face said, "Mrs. Magstadt, you mean we are going to learn bad words?"

It took me awhile to figure out the connection. Ah! Then I got it! *Cursive... cursing.*

65. I got the biggest kick out of these:

"I told my mom I wanted another brother but she said, 'I can't handle another kid.'"

"*Banana* is kinda a fun word to spell ya know? All those a's—you can't go wrong."

"My favorite cat got run over before I was born."

Student: "Mrs. Magstadt, I have a mosquito bite as big as a golf ball!"
Me: "Really? Let me see it."
Student: "You really can't see it that good."
Me: "Why not?"
Student: "I don't know."
"My dad made a lot of $10 bills on the copy machine. He does it all the time."

***

66. I got the biggest kick out of these too:

Student: "Sometimes when I talk too much, I have to stop and breathe."
Yuh think?

Comment made to me, "Yup, you *may* be right, Mrs. Magstadt."

"Mrs. Magstadt, can you speak Italian-American?"
"No, I don't think so."
"I can."
"Say something for me in Italian-American."
"Itza gonn-a be-a very hot-a today-a."

Student: Have you ever had dip *deesh* pizza? It's really *really* good."

Comment: "I'm not allergic, I'm just a picky eater."

"Mrs. Magstadt, did you know that nothing is impossible? Except for one thing—an impossibility—now, that's *impossible*!"

***

67. I commented about a picture that the class was looking at by saying, "That's about the cutest thing I've ever seen!"

Someone answered back, "Not our faces?"

68. The class was helping me clean and straighten our classroom library the last day of school and I said, "Wow, you guys are so much help!"

Student: "That's what we're here for!"

***

69. Student: "Mrs. Magstadt, what are you gonna do without us all summer, when you have nothing to do?"

Another student: "She's gonna play with Grace (*my dog*)—don't you know!"

Yup, that's all I am going to do!

***

70. On the way to lunch all kinds of topics come up:

"You know the wedding I was at this weekend?"
Me: "Yes."
"They had two gardeners."
Me: "Two gardeners?"
"Yeah, ya know, like the bride wears. She wore two *gardeners*."
Me: "Oh, you mean *garters*, she wore two *garters*."

"My grandpa's dog is a professional."
Me: "Why do you say that?"
"I don't know, but my grandpa said he is a professional."
Me: "What is the dog's profession?"
Quizzical look. "I don't know."
Me: "If you are a professional, you are usually really good at something. What is the dog good at doing?"
"Maybe hunting. I think he is a professional hunter."

***

71. Talking about the months of the year, someone answered my question with the word *June*.
Student, all excited, says, "That's my dad's name, June."
Me: "It *is*?"
Student: "Yeah, __Junior, you know? *June* for short."

***

72. I told the kiddos they would not be having any cursive homework this weekend and I heard someone say, "All hail, Mrs. Magstadt! All hail, Mrs. Magstadt!"

73. This past week I asked the class, "What is the hardest thing about being a kid?

Being too short to go on rides.
The hardest thing is homework.
The hardest thing is having to do chores.
The hardest thing is having to eat all your food.
The hardest thing is that you don't get your way.
Always being told what to do.
I think the hardest thing is speaking in a different language.
The hardest thing is having to wait for things.
The hardest thing is not being able to reach things.
The hardest thing is not talking. *I can attest to this one.*
The hardest thing is not being old enough for some things.
The hardest things are not being able to drive, use the stove, and having to go to bed at a certain time.

***

74. Student: "I couldn't live without television!"
Me: "Of course you could! What does TV have that you need in order to live?"

Student: "The weather report?" *That kid must be a farm kid!*

***

75. While I was on recess duty, a little first grader came up and said, "See my shoes?"

"Yes, I do. They sure are cute!"

"They're dancing shoes."
"They are? Then you should be dancing!"

The first grader answered shyly, "Noooooooo."

Me: "I think those dancing shoes want to dance!" So I grabbed her hands and twirled her around a few times while she giggled and smiled. "You sure are a good dancer!"

First grader: "Yup, it's the shoes."

A few days later, the same little first grader, "Do you like my shoes?"

"Yes, I do, but where are your dancing shoes today?"

"These are my walking shoes. I just want to walk."

76. Me: "So who is the smartest person in your family?"

Student: "Could be my dad, but Mom won't let him."

***

77. Thursday I told the kids that I was going to my uncle's 90th birthday party on Saturday. All kinds of questions followed:
What's his name?
Where does he live?
Will there be cake?
Will you play games?
Me: "I'm sure he'll have a cake, but I don't know if there will be games or not."
Will he have 90 candles? Whoa, that's a *lot* of candles.

A discussion followed regarding how to light so many candles and keep them going long enough to blow out. One student had the answer, "Have 'em use a blowtorch!"

***

78. When arriving at school in the morning, most of the second graders can get their outerwear

off and backpacks unpacked in five minutes or less except for one little guy. It can take him up to 15 minutes, mostly because he likes to visit with anybody and everybody who walks by. In an effort to get him to move a little faster I said, "Good morning. I bet you are going to really hurry for me this morning, right?"

His reply: "I don't think so. I'm kinda tired today."

So much for that strategy.

***

79. Interesting comments heard this week:

Mrs. Magstadt, you look good sitting in a little chair!

I like math more than cursive.

I liked cursive but now it's hurting me. *Tired hands.*

Cursive is like the best thing to happen to me lately.

Mrs. Magstadt, did you just roll your eyes at me? *Oops, probably!*

Kids are always smarter than teachers, sometimes. Mrs. Magstadt, you crack us up.

If they only knew how much they crack ME up!

Chocolate makes you smarter.

***

80. Student: "My dad says I'm annoying. Yeah, I bug my dad a lot. I'm with him too much. I talk too much."

Me: "Do you bug your dad on purpose?"

Student: "Sometimes, but sometimes it just happens."

***

81. This is how one student started telling me what turned out to be a very long story:

"Mrs. Magstadt, you know, me and my sister and

my cousin and my other cousin and my other cousin, well, I'm not sure if we're cousins, but he's like almost a cousin ..."

***

82. One day this week a student asked me, "Mrs. Magstadt, how old is God?" *First time I'd been asked that!*

I simply said I didn't know, so someone said, "Look in those books over there!" (Encyclopedias)

Of course someone said, "Google it, Mrs. Magstadt. Google it!"

I couldn't do that but I did hear this discussion. "God is older than the world."

"He was here before the dinosaurs."

"He was born at Christmas so he's not too old."

"It was his birthday on Christmas, like not his born-day."
"He's the oldest person *ever*!"

Kids really crack me up!

Since they didn't get an answer from me, I heard them ask our school counselor, Tina Miller, the same question!

***

83. Returning from the library one day, a little girl scurried up to talk to me, all excited, and she said, "Mrs. Magstadt, did you know the slowest moving animal on earth is a *slob*?"

***

84. One day last week, our bus driver, Pauline, had one student left to drop off. As they got close to his home, he saw a cat in the ditch and said, "Hey, that's our cat, Buster!"

When Pauline looked, she saw the cat had a can stuck on its head so she stopped the bus and was able to pick the cat up, no problem. She couldn't get the can off, so she said. "We'll take the cat to your house and get some help.

So the cat sat beside Pauline on the floor of the bus and never moved. When they got to his house, the little boy ran and got his mom to help."
    Pauline held the cat, and the mom twisted carefully on the can. It was an Alpo can!

When the can came off and the cat saw it was people that were helping him, he went ballistic, and Pauline ended up with some good scratches. As the cat took off, the little boy said, "Hmm, guess that wasn't our cat."

***

85. Second grader: "Mrs. Magstadt, what are consonants again?"

Me: "All the letters that aren't vowels are called *consonants*."
Second grader: "I knew that once. It just popped out of my head, I guess."

Me: "That happens!"

***

86. Out of the blue one day:

One student: "Mrs. Magstadt, I got a shot in my mouth July 17th and it still hurts."

Second student: "Me and my sisters all got beetle shots before we moved here."

Me: "A what?"

Second student: "A beetle shot."

Me: "Do you mean a measles shot?"

Second student: "Nope. A BEETLE shot. In the arm. It hurt."

Me: "What does a beetle shot do?"

Second student: "It hurts."

Me, trying again: "What is it for?"

Second student: "I don't know, nobody told me."

***

87. Learning about proper and common nouns:

Me: "Tell me why that isn't a proper noun."

Student: "It's not *pacific* enough."

88. After teaching all these years, I know a *lot* of second-grade-type jokes and riddles. It's not often I don't know the answers, but one little boy got me with the following joke:

"What mouse stands on two legs?"

Me, thinking, *oh, this is easy*: "Mickey Mouse?"

"Yup, what ducks stands on two legs?"

Me: "That must be Donald Duck!"

Second grader, grinning from ear to ear: "Nope! All ducks stand on two legs!"

***

89. Every once in a while someone forgets their homework:

I actually accidentally forgot to put it in my backpack.
My mom forgot to put it in my backpack.
I brought it back, but I didn't do it.
I did it, but I think I left it at home, on the bus, in our car, on the table, at Grandma's house!
I don't know where it is!

Was I supposed to take that home?
I forgot to do it.
We *had* homework?

***

90. Last Friday one of my students brought me a caramel roll. Yum!

On Monday another student brought me a caramel roll! Yum!

Lo and behold, today (Tuesday), another student brought me a caramel roll! Yum!

Does a caramel roll a day keep the *grumpies* away? I think so! Those kids have it figured out!

***

91. After having taken a bathroom break, a second grader popped back into the room, all smiles, and said, "Gee, I love this school!"

Me: "Why is that?"

Second grader: "All the teachers say *hi* to me! Everybody likes me!"

Another second grader: "They're teachers, they *have* to like you!"

92. Second grader to Mrs. Magstadt: "I read for 12 hours last night!"

Me: "Really?"

"Yup, I stayed up till nine."

***

93: Fun comments:

"Did you know if a volcano interrupts, it can make an island?"

"Mrs. Magstadt, get ready to be amazed!"

"Mrs. Magstadt, you should be on *America's Funniest Teachers!*"
"Why?"
"Cuz you crack me up!"

***

94. One of my little girls was totally engrossed reading a book when all of a sudden her hand shot up in the air. "Mrs. Magstadt, I found a contraption."

Me, wondering what she was talking about:

"What did you find?"

"A contraption!"

Me: "Well, you better show me that."

So she excitedly brought her book up and pointed to the word ... *don't*.

***

95. A small reading group and I were reading a book about a young girl who finds a book written by her great-great-great-grandmother when she was the same age as the girl is now. The grandmother wrote about what was happening in her life at the time and about her family. So I asked, "Does anyone know what you call a book that you write in every day and tell about your life, feelings, etc.?"

Before I could even blink, one little guy piped up, deadly serious, "I know, I know, it's a *diarrhea*!"

This was followed by a discussion of *diarrhea* vs. *diary*—and lots of giggles!

96. "Mrs. Magstadt, can I show you something?"
"Sure."

"Look at this."

Student pulls up his pant leg to show me a huge bandage on his left knee.

"Oh my, what happened?"

"No wait, look at this too."

He pulled his right pant leg and showed me a huge bandage on that knee as well.

"What happened?"

"A treadmill set at 7.2 miles per hour, that's what happened!"

***

97. When I was dismissing the kids after lunch, I noticed one group was reaching the length of the table, like they were measuring it. When I asked them what they were doing, one of them answered, "We're talking about nukes, and I'm showing them how big they are."

Me: "Oh, really? So … what is a *nuke*?"

Nobody could tell me except one little boy who came up to me and whispered, "They have them on an army base, and they use them for attacking stuff. And *trust me*, it's no good when they have to use them."

Amen to that!

***

98. One afternoon had gone particularly fast for all of us and when recess time came so quickly, we were all surprised.

One little guy said, "Time goes fast when you're having fun."

Followed by another who said, "Yup, time goes fast when you get as old as we are."

***

99. I gave each of the kids a valentine with a two dollar bill and a one dollar coin inside for Valentine's Day. They were hyped up and pretty tickled to receive that! Among the comments I

heard were:

"Where did you get all this money?"

"I am NEVER going to spend this, EVER!"

"I am going to show this to my grandpa and he is going to want it!"

"Mrs. Magstadt, how could you afford this?"

"Mrs. Magstadt, this is three dollars! Three *whole* dollars!"

"How did you find so many two dollar bills?"
Me: "I got them at the bank."
"The bank has *that kind* of money?"

***

100. Can you decipher the mysterious second grade spellings of the words below?

batree
kunfuzed
difurnt
adishun

spostto
durekshuns
recktngul
motsarela
insex
sekunt

***

101. A few years ago we were on a field trip to Jamestown and stopped at the Buffalo Village on the hill. My group immediately took off to see the statue of the World's Largest Buffalo. As we got to the buffalo and were standing underneath, looking up, a little guy pointed and said, very seriously, "Those are his testicles, right, Mrs. Magstadt?"

"Yup, you're right."

***

102. It's been quite a while, but the highway patrolman used to come in and do presentations on seatbelt safety for the kids. After their introduction and a video about the importance of using seatbelts, it was time for a question and answer session.

"Why are you wearing a gun?"

"Is it a real gun?"

"How many people have you shot?"

"Did anybody ever shoot you?"

"How fast does your car go?"

"A cop stopped my mom for speeding once."

"Mine, too."

"My grandpa got stopped and he was mad."

"My dad won't wear his seatbelt."

"My dad throws beer cans out the window, but I tell him not to do that."

Let's just say that having a seatbelt safety presentation is highly entertaining! And yes, all of the above comments were made—and there were even more that I decided not to share!

103. Some questions and comments for the week:

"Mrs. Magstadt, I'm a vegetable garden."
"Are caves real?"
"Are kings real?"
"Do you know what a cow pie is?"
"I caught a piranha at a lake by Bismarck."
Mrs. Magstadt, are diamonds real?"
Me: "Yes."
"Do you have a diamond?"
Me: "Yes, here on my engagement and wedding rings."
"Are they real?"
Me: "I'm pretty sure they are."
"You better check. They might be fake, you know."

"Mrs. Magstadt, are you Catholic?"
Me: (I always have to ask this) "What does *Catholic* mean?"
"It means you love God, Mary, and Jesus."
"Well, I love God, Mary, and Jesus, but I'm Lutheran."
Student: "So is that like a Catholic?"

104. The class was editing the following sentence:

The leafs beginned to turn orange red and brown in october
They do a great job finding the errors, and sometimes they just change it up their own way.

The leaves started to turn colors in October.

There's more than one way to fix a sentence!

***

105. Two little boys came in from recess all excited because they had so much fun together. One little guy was just giggling as he was telling me how they were chasing each other up and down the snow piles. While running, the one fell down and the other fell over the top of him.

"And you know what, Mrs. Magstadt? He kicked me right in the N-U-T-S!"

When you don't want to get in trouble—just spell.

106. As we lined up in the hallway before heading to lunch, one of my little guys scrunched up his face in pain and groaned a little bit. When I asked him what was wrong he said, "My leg hurts."

So I asked if he had fallen and hurt it. "Nope it's just one of those things. I can't remember what it's called. Something about a horse."

Me, smiling: "Do you mean a *charley horse?*"

"Yup, yup, that's it!"

***

107. We have been studying and practicing counting money recently, and some of the kids have been using their parents' change at home for extra practice. One little guy piped up, "My brother has a really BIG jar as tall as me to put money in—but we can't use it cuz it's his Vegas money."

***

108. As the kids returned all rosy-cheeked from recess outside, I asked them if it was pretty cold out. Some said, "Yes, freezing!" And others said,

"It's not very cold at all."

One little gal added, "Don't worry about us, Mrs. Magstadt. We're all okay because we're warm-blooded!"

***

109. When kids accidentally call me *Mom* or *Grandma*, I usually just say, "Okay, I'll be your mom," or "I'll be your grandma."

One little guy calls me Mom a lot and the last time he did he said, "When I'm in school, I call you *Mom*, and when I'm home, I call my mom *Mrs. Magstadt*! Why do I do that?"

Me: "Must be because we look so much alike!"

He looked at me thoughtfully with his face all scrunched up and said, "No, not really. I think it's because we spend too much time together!"

***

110. Just out of the blue, "Mrs. Magstadt, do you know what castrating is?"

"Sure do! Do you?"

"Yup."

"Can you tell me what it is?"

Student, smiling, thinking hard ... long pause, "Well ..." *longer pause*

Me: "How about I tell you and you see if I'm right?"

(Look of relief) "Yeah, okay."
Me: "It's when you turn a bull into a steer, right?"

Student, nodding his head: "I didn't want to tell you the DISGUSTING way!"

***

111. Interesting comments:

"I just LOVE wholesome!"
"Someone licked this ruler!"
"Mrs. Magstadt, are *you* wearing *sneakers*!"
"Can I give you a hug?"
"I lost my glove three times today but I found it once!"

112. I love how second graders spell! Can you read the word below?

punchwashun
pukshwashen
ponchwashon
punuaishon
pachewachen
punkuation
And my favorite, punshoeashin
(*punctuation*)

One more word for you:

spgedy
sbgetee
spguti
spugetie
psgedee
spegee
spagety
And my favorite, spuhgeety
(*spaghetti*)

***

113. The following note was left for me by a substitute teacher one day this past week:

Mrs. Magstadt,

If you need a mental health day, you have my number.

Take care, hang in there, and God bless you, Woman!

***

114. You know it's been an extra cold winter with too many inside recesses when even second graders are asking, "When's it gonna get nice out?"

So when we changed to the March calendar I said, "The first day of spring is March 20th."

Someone said, "Good, only 20 days till winter is over."

If only that were true in North Dakota!

***

115. On a recent language paper, the second graders had to list five foods that are usually eaten for breakfast. Here are some of their answers with

their delightful spellings! *Do you eat this stuff for breakfast?*

walffels, touster stoutle, butter and jully, cerel, yogut

serell, bacun, sosuje, wofells, toest

skerabld eggs, fride eggs, tost, ciricle, otmie

bagl, cerul, putatoes, sasej, pandcakes,

surul, more surul, outmeel, toster shrutle, backen

cromcrols, serll, penet butter, oranj joose, gellee (caramel rolls?)

cereale, wawfuls, mufeens, banken, sussage

***

116. Finish this sentence: When I grow up I will definitely _____.

*be a farmer.
*be a doctor, a cheerleader and a hairstylist.
*be a singer and sing rock.
*be a policeman that drives a fast car.

*be a cowgirl.
*be a doctor so I can help people.
*play the guitar.
*be a zookeeper.
*run a farm.
*get a job.
*be in the army.
*be a woman.
*be rich.
*be married with kids.
*be myself.

***

117. Student: Mrs. Magstadt, do you know Justin Bieber?"

Me: No, I don't know him. Do you know him?"

Student: "Well, do you like to listen to him on the radio?"

Me: "No, I don't believe I have ever heard one of his songs. If I did, it wasn't on purpose."

Student: "Well, he just sings about love and girls, love and girls."

***

118: Student: Did I ever tell you that this is my lucky finger?"

(Pointing to the ring finger on his right hand.)

Me: "Noooo, how do you know it's lucky?"

Student: "Just if I touch something with this finger then *bam*—I get lucky!"

***

119. Explanation of Karma by a second grader: "Karma is if you do a bad thing, then a bad thing will happen back to you. If you do a good thing, then a good thing happens back."

Me: "So do you do bad or good things?"

Student: "I *try* to do mostly good things, you know, but it's hard."

Me: "It's even hard for grown-ups to do good things all the time."

Student: "Yes, I know, it's a difficult world."

120. Student, pointing to his paper: "I know why this isn't a proper noun, because it is not *specific* enough."

Me: "I love how you use the word *specific*."

Student: "I know lots of words. I even know *asteroid*."

***

121. Me, to student at my desk: "Sometimes you just amaze me!"

Student: "I know I do."

About a minute later he is at my desk again and he says, "I'm going to amaze you even more than I did before!" *And he did.*

***

122. The kiddos completed some well-known proverbs with their own bits of wit and wisdom so I will share a few with you!

Funny Stories

1. Scratch my back and I'll ...

*say thank-you!
*pay you!
*scratch your back, too!
*I'll be nice to you.
*pay you five dollars.
*give you a rose.
*make you a cake.
*scratch your CAT!

2. There is a time and a place for ...

*silliness.
*being funny.
*running.
*better actions.
*jumping on the bed.
*playing video games.
*lunch!
*IXL. (a computer math website)
*working for Mrs. Magstadt.
*playing with your dog (which is after you finish your homework).

3. What you don't know will ...

*be confusing.
*hurt you.
*maybe happen.
*come true.
*make you feel bad.
*appear!
*not kill you.
*probably be wrong!
*get you an eff! ("F")

4. The early bird catches …

*its food so it doesn't starve!
*its prey.
*no lateness.
*some fish.
*the flu.
*the bus
*more than a late bird.

5. Don't count your chickens before …

*the rooster crows.
*the mother lays the eggs.
*you cook the noodles.
*one in the morning.
*you kill them.

*you eat breakfast.
*Wednesday.
*you take your pajamas off.

***

123. You know winter has just been too long when a second grader can walk up to his teacher, point to his lips, not say a word, and the teacher pulls out the Chapstick, applies it to his finger, and keeps right on talking and teaching.

***

124. Student: "Mrs. Magstadt, what's up?"
Me: "I don't know, what *is* up?"

Student: "The ceiling! Get it? Do you get it, Mrs. Magstadt?"

***

125. "Mrs. Magstadt, can you roll your tongue like this?" (demonstration)

"Mrs. Magstadt, can you touch your nose with your tongue?" (demonstration)

Soon we had everybody trying to touch their nose

with their tongue.
"Can you bend your hand back really far like this and touch the top of your arm?"

"Try it, you should try it."

"Can you bend your elbow like this? I'm double-jointed. I have always been able to do this. I was born to do this."

"Can you cross your eyes?"

"Can you put your fingers like this?" (with a "V" in the middle)

"Can you make two v's with your fingers? Can you switch back and forth really fast between the v's? It's a talent—my mom says it runs in our family."

***

126. We are just about through learning how to write all the letters in cursive. (No one is happier than the teacher.) The kids always want me to look at letters they have written that look particularly awesome. A student had been up to

my desk a number of times to have me check out his writing. Evidently, he was pretty confident that he knew what he was doing as he came up again and said, "How does *this* one look?"

Me: "Great!"

Student, giggling: "I did it with my eyes closed. Should I do all of them with my eyes closed?"

Me: "Go right ahead."

***

127. While measuring objects in math, we turned to a page that had pictures of vegetables to measure, such as carrots, celery, etc. A little guy looked the page over and quickly said, "What? No rutabaga?"

***

128. The second graders were demonstrating their understanding of their vocabulary words by completing sentences:

*One thing I would describe as gigantic is...

the Capitol.
a monster truck.
a skyscraper.
the Statue of Liberty.
the Eiffel Tower.
an elephant.

*You would probably say yuck if you...

puke.
smell yucky.
stepped in mud.
fell in dog poop.
ate something gross.
saw something moldy.
ate something bad.
saw puke.
smell a stinky diaper.

*One thing that can ruin a good meal is...

PUKE!
accidentally spilling water into the food.
a face!
a food fight.
BROCCOLI!
your little sister.

moldy food.
rotten food.
dirt.
if it is burnt.
PUKE!

*You probably wouldn't embrace someone...

watering a plant.
if they are mean.
muddy.
that's a stranger.
if they are sick.
who hit you.
with a snake.
who calls you a name.

*One thing I think is incredible is...

a tightrope walker.
the first time you ride a bike.
a skyscraper.
how airplanes stay in the air.
cool creatures.
a waterpark!
cats doing tricks.

129. One of my duties while subbing this school year involved helping supervise the pre-kindergarteners through second graders during lunch. Let me tell you, that is an interesting experience. One of my favorite things is when a little one asks for "salad and wanch, please." Or when one little girl said, "Do you want to see me squeeze the guts out of this grape?"

And then there's this. Three little ones chewing away like crazy, then telling me, excitedly, that they found gum under the table!

***

130. Interesting comments this week by the kiddos:

"Technically, these words are really not in a-b-c order."

"This is obviously wrong ... obviously."

"This feels worse than when my dog died." (A comment about a classmate whose last day in our class was Friday.)

131. It's that time of the year:

"That mud is a bloomin' mess!" (the playground—Ugh, it is!)

"There's mud EVERYWHERE!"
"I didn't go in the mud on purpose. It just happened."

"My boots are SOAKED inside!"
Me: "How did that happen?"
"I *don't* know!"
Me: "Were you walking in the water?"
"Maybe, by accident."

"I am *sooo tireddd* of wearing snow pants!"
Me: "Well, this time of year they are mostly mud pants."
"I am *soooo tireddd* of wearing mud pants!"

***

132. The never-ending discussion regarding tackling at recess ended with me saying, "You

cannot tackle because you don't wear all the pads and other gear that football players wear for protection, okay? Let's just remember—it's touch football, not tackle."

Student: "Yes, remember—it's *recess* football, not *real* football."

***

133. Today I asked a little kindergarten boy whose birthday party he went to over Easter break. He smiled and said, "My Grandpa's."

"How old was he?"

He said, "59."

So, I had to ask, "Why were there only four candles on the cake?"

The little guy said, "Grandma said the fire department is busy enough." Then, he added, "Did you see me on Facebook?"

Part 3: Funny Stories from Duane Roth

DUANE ROTH
TAUGHT SIXTH GRADE 35 YEARS
SAME GRADE, SAME SCHOOL
BISMARCK, NORTH DAKOTA

Dr. Duane Roth has been a super-friend of Kevin Kremer's for many decades. The two first met at Mary College (University of Mary) in Bismarck when they were both starting a master's degree program through Northern State College in Aberdeen in 1976, and they've traveled through almost all of the 50 states together since then. If you ever have the pleasure to meet Duane, ask him about Hebron brick, head cheese, or the significance of the number 747. He will probably tell you *it's a long story*—but it's really not.

1: First Words Spoken

Helen Rask was a wonderful teacher and friend who taught at Pioneer Elementary School in Bismarck. One year, Helen taught a boy who hadn't spoken one word since the beginning of the school year. Two months had gone by and Helen was worrying that something was wrong with him. Then one day at school he went to the boys' bathroom. (The bathrooms were in the classroom at Pioneer.) Suddenly, the door flew open and the boy shouted, "Teacher! There is no sh-t paper in here!"

Those were the first words he spoke. Apparently, he had been satisfied up to that point.

2: You Mean a Big Thing Like YOU?

Helen Rask also told me a story about the little first grade girl that had an accident and didn't make it to the bathroom in time. Trying to console the little girl who was in tears, Helen told her about a time that it had happened to her, too.

The girl looked up at her teacher and said, "You mean a big thing like *you*?"

3: Sometimes You Can't Help Yourself

I had a girl in my classroom who never *ever* did anything wrong. One day we had a police officer speaking to our class. He was passing around some of his equipment. I was sitting at the back of the room. After looking at the handcuffs, I passed them to the girl in front of me that never *ever ever* did anything wrong. She looked at the handcuffs and passed them to the boy in front of her. The boy put his hand in one of the cuffs ... and the girl that *never never never ever ever ever* did anything wrong reached up and snapped the handcuff shut on the boy!

The officer saw the situation and said, "Oh no! I forgot to bring the key!" Then he paused a few seconds and said he was just kidding.

After school I asked the girl, "Why did you snap those handcuffs shut?"

She replied, "It was just *sooo* tempting."

4: The Old Mimeograph Machine

I ran off copies of a worksheet on the mimeograph machine in the teachers' lounge. Do you remember the master copy with that distinctive purple color? Usually I would throw that copy away in the teachers' lounge. This particular time, though, I forgot and threw it away in the trash can in my classroom. Later in the day I noticed a curious student reach down in the trash can to see what that purple sheet was all about. He got purple on his hand and then went to get a paper towel to wipe it off. By wiping with the paper towel, his whole hand became purple.

5: You Can't Beat Head Cheese

One day Sue Triska, the other sixth grade teacher at Pioneer School in Bismarck, was in my classroom before school started.

One of her students came into my classroom with something for me. It was a toothpick with something the size of a quarter on it.

I thanked him and asked him what it was. He said that it was some *head cheese* that he'd brought from home. I told him I would eat it later, and he left the room. I thought Sue was going to die from laughing! We went over to Sue's classroom, and that same student had brought her a toothpick with head cheese on it too!

6: You're FIRED!

Our principal, Wayne Granfor, was retiring and the teachers wanted to film a video of the school to give to him. As part of the video, they wanted all of the teachers and students in their classrooms. When they came into my classroom, I jumped up on a table and said, "Mr. Granfor, you can't fire me anymore!"

About a week later Mr. Granfor opened the classroom door and said, "You are fired!"—and closed the door.

My class just laughed.

7. I Patiently Wait

The first year I taught school, I had a Native American student named Carl, who was very quiet. After a while, when I knew I could kid around with Carl, I would say, "Carl, when are we going to talk?"

Carl would just smile. The whole year I kept saying, "Carl, when are we going to talk?" He would always smile.

The last week of school Carl wrote on a piece of paper for me, "Someday we will talk."

So I patiently wait for the day when Carl and I will talk.

8: Winnie Hoersch Fun

Winnie Hoersch taught at Pioneer Elementary in Bismarck for 35 years. She was a wonderful teacher. At Christmas she would take a razor blade, slice the tape, and then unwrap the presents she had received from her students to see what she was getting. Then she would wrap them all up so it looked just like she'd never done a thing. How do I know? Because I saw her doing that!

9: He Wrote a Whole Page

I had this student who had Asperger syndrome. One time he had a creative writing assignment and he turned in his paper. I thought, *Wow! He's written a whole page*! I started to read it, but I couldn't make sense of even the first sentence. I called him back to me and told him to read his story to me. He looked at the paper and said, "I can't read it either." We both burst out laughing.

10: It Was a Delicate Situation Wrestling a Girl

Grade school wrestling in Bismarck had a few tournaments where other grade schools participated. There was a third or fourth grade boy that I knew because I had his sisters in my room at one time, and this boy had to wrestle a girl. During the match he got her down on her back and was going to pin her—but he didn't know where to touch her, so he used the thumb and forefinger of both of his hands and gently pushed down on her collar bones to pin her. I thought that was the funniest thing.

11: Minister Referee

We were invited out to our friends' house for supper. One of the guests was a retired minister. When he had been a minister, he had also been a basketball referee. He told us about one time when someone from the crowd hollered, "**I hope he's a better preacher!**"

12: Wayne Triska Story

I was talking to Wayne Triska, and he was telling me about working in Winnie Hoersch's room with a student that was vision impaired. The student was learning braille. The student turned in a page of creative writing in braille. Wayne would take the paper and write the letters above the braille for the teacher.

Wayne was feeling good about the assignment until he tried to convert it. He could not make out one thing. Winnie said to him, "If you turned it around, it might help." He had the paper upside down!

13: Bubble Wrap

This isn't that funny, but we had fun doing this. Once at school I had some bubble wrap, it would go *pop* when you squeezed it. I selected two students to take the bubble wrap up to the office. The secretary turned on the intercom speaker to just our room. The students got to pop all of the bubbles on the intercom into our room. In the classroom we got the biggest kick out of listening to the bubbles pop.

14: Please Pass the Mouth Wash

I finished presenting the lesson and was walking around the room helping students. This boy raised his hand, and I went over to help him. The boy told me, "Someone in this row has bad breath."

15: Chalkboard Wisdom

Each week, I wrote down a little something for the week. That particular week it was, "Doing your best is more important than being the best." One boy said to me, "Isn't it great doing your best *and* being the best!"

16: The Big Words

At parent-teacher conferences I was explaining to a parent about the vocabulary words. She said, "Oh, those are those big words!" So, for the rest of the year in class we had a nickname for vocabulary—*The Big Words*.

17. The F-Word

A kindergarten teacher at Pioneer told me this. A little kindergarten girl came in from recess and told the teacher that a boy in their class said the F-word. Privately the teacher talked with the boy and found out that he said *sh-t!*

18: Ginny Eck

Ginny used to tell me this story. One noon when she was teaching at Dorothy Moses School in Bismarck, she had to go home to check on some cows that were calving. She was speeding home and got stopped by the police. Ginny told the officer, "Please write up the ticket. I have to check on my cows. I'll pick up the ticket on the way back."

Ginny came back and picked up her ticket and went back to school to teach the afternoon.

I don't know if she knew the officer, but knowing Ginny, it probably wouldn't have made a difference.

19: Donald Dook

I had a girl from Bosnia in my class. I had flash cards to help her with her English. The cards had a picture with a word on it. I would flash the card with the word *car* on it, say *car*, and she would say *car*. I would flash the card with the word *dog* on it, I would say *dog*, and she would say *dog*. I would flash the card with the word *duck* on it, say *duck*, and she would say **dook**.

The next year I had a boy from Bosnia from a different family. I would go through the same routine. When I got to *duck* he would say *dook*. I would say, "No, it is *duck*."

"Yes," he said. "Dook."

So, I guess it is *dook*. Donald Dook.

20: Go Get Her!

I had a boy in the sixth grade that had a sister in kindergarten. She would often take off during the school day and run home.

One day the boy in my class looked out the

window and shouted, "My sister is running home!"

I said, "Go get her!"

He took off running out of the classroom. A while later he came back and told me he'd caught her about two blocks from school and brought her back.

21: The Talking Calculator

I was in graduate school taking statistics, and we had a blind student in class from one of the Arab countries. He had a talking calculator. I thought, *Wow, we will be able to hear the answers during a test.*

To my surprise, the calculator talked in Arabic.

I was sitting beside that same student in class, and I noticed he had his eyes closed. I thought, *He must be really listening and getting into this class.* Then I realized he was sleeping.

22. Money Was Tight

In high school after a football game, we came back into the locker room. Our tackle opened his fist and told us he'd found a quarter which he had held in his fist the entire football game.

During one of our high school reunions, we reminded him of that story. He said, "No, that isn't right." It was *two* quarters that he had found and held in his fist the whole football game.

Hey, money was tight way back then!

23. English Teacher Fun

You have to remember this happened in a small town. After football practice the team was walking back to the gym, and the English teacher had her car parked there. I have no idea whose idea this was, but we lifted the back end of the car and put some blocks under it.

The team went back over by the field and nonchalantly watched what would happen. The teacher came out, got in her car, put it in reverse, and nothing happened. She did this three times and the tires would just spin. She got out of her car and looked bewildered. We went over there and confessed, then we took the blocks out. Our English teacher was such a good sport, and she just laughed and laughed.

24. You Deserve a Ticket

I had a blind boy in class. He wanted to be the policeman in our simulated town because his brother was the policeman when he was in my room. I told my teaching partner, Sue, that I can't have him be the policeman and gave him the candy store. It always bothered the boy that he had to have the candy store instead of being the policeman.

The next year I thought I would invite the blind student back to be the policeman for a day in our town. I contacted the boy's teacher and explained the situation and she agreed. She also contacted the Bismarck Police Department, and they had a patrol car pick up my former student at the middle school and drive him over to our school.

He finally got to be policeman in our town, and he gave me a much-deserved ticket for not letting him be policeman the previous year!

25. Just Jump!

The hallway in our school had a portion coming down from the ceiling. The students would like to jump up and touch it. I told my class at the beginning of the year that we were not going to jump up and touch that because it would get dirty and the custodians would have to clean it.

When we would line up to go down the hallway, I had this boy that would look up at the ceiling, look at me, and give me a grin. This went on the whole year. On the last day of school, I called him out into the hallway. I told him to run, jump up, and touch the ceiling. He couldn't believe it, and after he was done, we just looked at each other and grinned.

26. The Hand and the Trash Can

I never asked him to do it, but we had a custodian that would empty the trash can all the time. I had my trash can located by the door. During the day I would see this hand reach around the door, grab the trash can, empty it into another container in the hallway, and put it back. We would never see his body, just the hand. The trash can was never that full, and he did it so quietly it never bothered the class. He did this several times during the day—the hand would grab the trash can and empty it. When he cleaned the room and emptied the trash can at the end of the day, it never was that full. The funny thing is—when we got a new custodian, it bothered me when the trash can was full.

27. That's Warming-Up Your Car!

Before there were car starters, some teachers would start their cars at noon on those real cold North Dakota days. Then they'd let the engine run for a while, just to make sure it would start after school. One of our teachers did that one day. At the end of the school day she noticed that she'd forgotten to turn off her car. It had run all afternoon. The street was covered with snow, but around her car was a big circle of a dry pavement. Her car was parked right outside of her classroom so she could see it, but sometimes teachers get really busy.

28. The Good Lord Will Do It

Our principal, John Wanser, would tell our custodian Jim to go out and shovel the snow off the sidewalks. Jim would respond by saying, "The good Lord put it there, and He will take it away."

Mr. Wanser would reply, "Until He does—go out and shovel the sidewalk."

29. Terrific Dean Turner

Professor Dean Turner, a terrific teacher and person, taught Philosophy of Education at the University of Northern Colorado. One day, he gave us some questions to think about, and he said we would discuss them during the next class. Someone in our group thought we should go over to the library because Dr. Turner had written some books, and we could possibly find the answers to some of the questions in them.

The next day in class we were discussing the questions. Suddenly, Dr. Turner got this big grin on his face and said, "I see some people have been reading my books!"

30. The Simple Things Can Be the Best

We had this cleaning lady at our school that would clean the sinks and the tops of the desks in the classroom. I always enjoyed talking to her. When she got to the student's desk nearest my desk, she would start talking then look down and wipe the desk, look up, talk, and wipe on the desk again. She would wipe on the same spot about five or six times. All of a sudden she would say, "I have to get going or I'll never get finished!"

31. Is it a Real Diamond?

I had a parent-teacher conference with a father that had been one of my students. He told me the story about when he was in the fifth grade in the room right beside my room, and a girl had claimed that the ring she was wearing had a diamond in it. None of the fifth graders believed her and told her to prove it.

The classrooms had a window in the door, and the girl scratched the ring on the window and it left a scratch mark. Wow! That convinced the kids that it was a real diamond!

After the parent-teacher conference we went next door and checked the window, and sure enough, there was a scratch on the window after all of those years.

32. Where's Waldo?

Waldo was a fancy bookmark that I bought in a bookstore. I started hiding it, and the class would look for him each morning. Sue Triska and I would switch classes, and I would teach her class math. The funny thing was, when her class came through my classroom door, they immediately started searching for Waldo. They wouldn't be paying attention to where they were walking—their eyes would be searching for Waldo.

I would wait till everyone was in the room and give everyone a chance then I'd call on a student to point to Waldo. Once in a while Sue and I would just switch classrooms, but the first thing they had to know was—where was Waldo in my classroom?

One morning my class couldn't find Waldo. The secretary called into our room and said Waldo had called, and he was sick and would not be coming to school today.

33. Doing an Experiment on the Professor!

We had a great psychology professor in the master's degree program at Northern State College in Aberdeen, South Dakota. I'll never forget when he told us about losing all of the research for his doctoral thesis in a campus fire, and he was never able to finish his doctoral program. That was before the days of Xerox machines and flash drives.

Anyway, he told another story about when his class did an experiment on *him* without his knowledge! When the professor was on the left side of the room, the class would be very attentive and listen. When he moved to the right side of the room, they didn't pay attention. Well, he ended up spending most of the lecture on the left side of the room.

After class, the students told the professor what they'd done, and he told them how much he enjoyed their experiment!

34. The kid REALLY got into it!

I had my sixth graders collect some insects in a jar. They would research the insect and write some facts about it on an index card.

We would go up to the first grade room, get into small groups, and show-and-tell them about the insect.

The first grade teacher came over to me laughing and said, "I've never seen anything like it!" I didn't know that one of my sixth graders *really* got into it. He had brought a dissecting kit and charts, and he was acting like a doctor.

Part 4: Funny Stories from Kevin Kremer

I thought I could *maybe* come up with 25 stories for the book—but it wasn't that hard to think of 50.

Thanks to all my teachers and students—plus all those kids in all the schools I visited as an author—for making me laugh!

Story 1: You've Got to be Kidding me!

I taught an interdisciplinary Super Bowl unit in my classroom during the week of the championship game each year. At the end of the week, the kids would predict the winner and the score of the big game. The best predictor received a signed football the Monday morning after the Super Bowl.

In 1990, the football was signed by a former student, an excellent football player who had visited my classroom earlier in the year. That year, one of the girls in my class wrote down 50-0 for her prediction, and she picked the 49ers to beat the Broncos. Because she had a fun personality and could give out as much guff as she took, I gave her a rough time about this *many* times, and she answered by just laughing and saying, "You'll see!"

I replied, "I'll give you an extra $20 (I almost said $1,000) plus a trip to Happy Joe's Pizza *besides* the football if you win with such a RIDICULOUS (I might have said *stupid*) prediction! It will simply NOT happen! I *guarantee* it!" (I must confess I was a Broncos fan at the time, too, largely because I went to graduate school at the University of Northern Colorado in Greeley where they trained.)

Well, the next Monday, and for many days after that, I treated the girl with the RIDICULOUS prediction with the reverence she deserved—and I also paid her off! The final score: 49ers, 55 ... Broncos, 10!

STORY 2: NO MORE ENGLISH LEATHER!

My first year of teaching, I taught math and science to 75 fifth graders in Rugby, North Dakota. As the day before Christmas vacation arrived, I knew I was the first male teacher most of these students ever had, and I wondered what kinds of gifts I might get from the kids. It was quite a surprise! More than 30 bottles of English Leather, Brut, and Old Spice—but only one bottle of wine! After that year, I used to semi-jokingly remind my students when they asked me what I wanted for Christmas, "Please don't get me anything for Christmas, but if you must, just remember—I wear XL sweatshirts!"

I probably should have mentioned something about the students pitching together for *one* sweatshirt, because one year, I got 17 XL sweatshirts!

Story 3: Some Records Were Meant to be Broken

The first day of school I always mentioned to the kids, "If you ever feel ill and need to head to the bathroom, please don't bother to raise your hand and ask for permission—just get there as fast as you can. For many years I added, with a chuckle, "No one has ever gotten sick (puked) in my classroom all the years I've taught." That was a fact.

Many years passed. One day, one of the sweetest girls I've ever taught got out of her chair, ran for the door, opened it up … but she didn't quite make it completely out of the door before she puked partly in the classroom and partly out in the hall. When she came back to the classroom later, feeling much better, she looked at me with a partial smile-partial grimace and said, "I'm so sorry I ruined your record, Dr. Kremer."

Story 4: Pennies from Heaven

One spring, I noticed the large number of kindergarteners and first graders playing in the area covered with sand on the playground at our school. It reminded me of the great Mandan Elks and Mandan Rural Fire Departments picnics when I was a kid when we dug in the sawdust for pennies. I loved that!

Well, I had a huge jar full of pennies at home, so I thought I'd give the kids a little taste of that fun. Very early one morning, when I usually went to school, still in the dark, I carefully poured a bunch of pennies and a few nickels and dimes in the sand and mixed them all around, burying them. Later in the morning, before school started, I walked out on the playground to see what was happening. It was like bringing back my old memories. The kids were having a blast—much like I used to have at those old picnics!

Story 5: The Tear Gas Incident of 1964

The details of this incident are still not completely clear to me, but I sure do have a lot of dreams about it. This is how I remember it.

I know it was early December of 1964, and someone had broken into the office at Mandan Junior High at night—I'm guessing for the small amount of money kept in there from hot lunch and stuff. The police thought the criminals were in the old steam tunnels that ran throughout the old building so they filled them with tear-gas, hoping to flush the criminals out. School was cancelled the next day.

The day after that, we came back into the school, and there was still tear gas lingering, affecting many of us. My eyes hurt, and I wasn't the only one coughing and tearing up throughout the day. It was really uncomfortable!

Did they ever catch the criminal or criminals? I don't know. Over the decades my dreams involving the incident have changed little—sometimes the cloud of tear gas in the large study hall is thicker than others. Sometimes in my dream I ask a teacher, "What the *heck* are we doing in school!?" Other times, someone like John Wayne will show up in the tear gas dream and make a comment about the strange conditions in the school.

STORY 6: THE BOOMING VOICE OF LEFTY FARIS!

His voice calls out to me 50 years later—and it always makes me laugh! It's the one voice from my school days that stands out above all others—the deep BOOMING voice of Lefty Faris!

Lefty was Mandan High School's athletic director and my government teacher when I was attending Mandan High, but he had been an outstanding football coach when I was much younger. My dad used to take us to all the home football games at the field that would eventually be named Lefty Faris Field.

The voices of John Facenda, James Earl Jones, and Barry White had nothing on Lefty Faris' voice. It was deep, commanding—maybe a little raspy. He needed no microphone at crowded athletic events in our large gymnasium. **"Would everyone please move to the center so we can get more people in here!"** His voice **boomed**—and everyone moved.

People loved to imitate his voice … and good imitations always led to laughter. He said RASSLING for the word *wrestling*. "Hey BOYS!" was another common *Lefty phrase* to mimic.

My senior year in his government class, I got to be his errand boy. "Hey, KREMER! Do me a favor!" he'd say. "Would you go down to my office and get the red notebook on my desk." Often he'd put significant pressure on my collarbone with his left hand as he was giving me instructions, so I'd be grimacing as he was talking.

I'm sorry I never heard Lefty sing. I can only imagine him singing the "Mandan Fight Song." He would definitely be more entertaining than Harry Caray singing "Take Me Out to the Ballgame." I'm going to try to sing it with Lefty's voice right now! If you knew Lefty, I'll bet you can hear me.

Here's to Mandan, here's to Mandan
Let us boost our dear old high!
Raise the song both loud and long
And let it reach up to the sky.
Loyal classmates, loyal classmates,
We depend on each of you,
Prove to our old high that
we are one and all true blue!
Let's give a rah! rah! rah! rah!
Mandan High is on the floor today.
Let's give a rah! rah! rah! rah!
Team! And cheer them on in every way.
Let's give a rah! rah! rah! rah!
Black and white, don't let our colors fall!
For we are with you every freshman, sophomore, junior, senior ... One and all!

Story 7: I'll Give You $10

I had a high school history teacher named Mr. Vickers who used to make tests that would challenge *anyone*. Then he would add some bonus questions that he thought were almost impossible to answer correctly—questions that might include some small, minute detail from a photo in the textbook or some fact that he'd shared in one of his lectures. I loved the challenge, and it helped me prepare for my toughest college teachers.

Occasionally I offered the same type of challenge to the fifth and sixth graders I taught, but I used money and good food as an added incentive. I'd say things like, "There's no way anyone will get a perfect paper on this next history test! It's way too hard. If it happens, I've got $10 for anyone that does it."

I still remember one of the kids at Highland Acres Elementary in Bismarck who met the challenge and got every question right plus the five bonus questions.

After I handed back his test, he said, "There's a model of a ship that costs ten dollars that I want to buy. Could we go get it in your Camaro after school?"

Story 8: What is this SHEEEET?

Mandan High's Spanish teacher was an incredible man. He had been a lawyer in Cuba and had escaped the island and certain death at the hands of Fidel Castro. He was an excellent teacher, but some of the duties and intricacies of the teaching profession were new to him.

One day during class, someone knocked at the door of the classroom, and he answered the door. Someone from the office handed him a sheet of paper, and our teacher looked at it with a quizzical expression on his face.

"What is this *sheet*?" he asked, with his distinctive accent.

It sounded a lot like a more vulgar expression "What is this sh-t?"—at least that's what many of us high schoolers heard.

After that, there were many people around high school asking the question "What is this *sheet*?" I still ask that question today.

Story 9: Fake Classroom Visitor from Australia

This particular sixth grade class had been a real challenge for me. They had definitely tired me out by the end of the school year. I thought it was time to play a little joke on them to conclude the school year.

Andrew was a friend of my sister Robin's, and he was a precocious high school kid with many talents. I'd watched him become an excellent actor in high school plays with creativity and personality like you wouldn't believe! I thought I would play a little joke on my sixth graders using Andrew as my accomplice.

This was my plan. I invited lots of classroom visitors in throughout the year, and I thought Andrew could come to class and act as if he were a foreign exchange student from Australia. I told Andrew my plan, and he loved the idea.

Andrew showed up on time and came into the classroom with a boomerang in hand. He played the part of Australian foreign exchange student so well, it was a little scary. His accent was good, and he answered all the questions the kids had unbelievably well. I kept totally serious the whole time, but inside, I was exploding with laughter.

Then something added to the fun. The third grade teacher, who was on a break and knew nothing about my fake visitor, came into the classroom during his visit. She got interested right away, even asked a question or two. She didn't suspect anything. (I never told her Andrew was an imposter.)

Soon, the kids asked Andrew to go out on the playground and demonstrate throwing the boomerang. I recall it really didn't go that well. I think the boomerang went over the fence, but Andrew had a good explanation for everything. Then he demonstrated a little of his soccer prowess, which was quite impressive.

The evening before the last day of school, I invited all the sixth graders to my parents' backyard in Mandan where I cooked them hamburgers on the grill. My parents and brothers and sisters helped serve them other great food too. ... Then I had Andrew show up! The kids were really excited to see him, and eventually he told them about our little joke.

Story 10: Pull-up Geese

The biggest challenge for most fifth and sixth graders with the President's Physical Fitness Award was doing the required number of pullups. I remember having that same challenge when I was going to school.

Because of this, I bought a pull-up bar mounted on a frame that was marked way down in price at Scheels in Bismarck and placed it in the back of my classroom. At the end of the day, students could go back and do pullups. Because the bar was quite high in the air for some kids, I spotted them all, just in case.

One of the girls in my class was a gymnast, a super-student, and a class leader. She gave 100% at everything. One day she was struggling on about her 25th pull-up, going for 26, giving it her best effort, straining, straining some more ... when the little girl emitted one of the loudest *farts* ever heard in the Northern Hemisphere. (Maybe this is a slight exaggeration.)

It was silent in the classroom for a millisecond after that explosion, and for some reason I said what I heard many times growing up in our large family when someone farted. "GEESE!"

The class had a good laugh, the girl turned a dark shade of red, and then I explained to the kids that this would be *our* funny story. I never heard anything more about it.

Story 11: The Blizzard of 1997

It was early April of 1997. There was some snow expected—but certainly not anything like a blizzard. There had been some sleet on Friday night, and now it was Saturday morning, and there was *serious snow* coming down. Then the wind picked up, making it much worse.

After doing a little shopping at nearby Kirkwood Shopping Center in Bismarck that morning, I decided to head to the school nearby in my truck and get some work done—never imagining the weather would become what it became. Hey! It was April!

When I got to the school and started working, I occasionally looked out the windows as the snow kept coming down and the wind kept picking up. I noticed my view out the windows was becoming blocked by snow—but I just kept on working, not even dreaming what would happen next.

An hour or so after that, I got a little concerned. I had a truck, and I was pretty sure I could travel three blocks to get home, but I needed to check things out. I went to the nearest exit and the door was impossible to open. Besides ice frozen around it, there was also a nice-sized snowdrift blocking it. I finally kicked the door open, stuck my head out, and realized this was a full-fledged blizzard, and I had a decision to make. Try to head home and probably get stuck—or stay in school.

I went to the exit nearest where my truck was parked and realized I probably wouldn't even make it out of the parking lot. That was the one time I wished my truck had four-wheel drive.

I went back in the building. I knew the biggest problem with staying in school would be trying to get any sleep. The best place for that would be on the uncomfortable sofa in the staff room, but no matter what, I decided staying in school was definitely the best option. Besides, I had so many school things to work on—plus the extensive halls would be great for running the five or six miles I ran every other day, and I loved shooting baskets in our gym.

I checked the refrigerator in the staff room. There were two large meat and cheese trays from Super Valu in there. The sixth graders were going to have a celebration of some kind on Monday. I loved meat and cheese trays, so I figured my food needs were taken care of. During the next several hours, I would eat everything on those trays, along with *many* Reese's peanut butter cups and other good things from the vending machine.

The thermostat was automatically set at a pretty low temperature for the weekend in the school, so that night I covered up with a bunch of clothes from the lost-and-found and tried to sleep. The sofa was even more uncomfortable than I imagined for my six-foot frame, and I also remember the smell of cheese from a stain on the sofa.

Unfortunately, the Coke and Pepsi vending machines in the staff room also made lots of noise, with the little coolers inside kicking in every few minutes or so, so sleep was almost impossible. During the weird dreams I got during sporadic periods of sleep, I actually had the Pepsi and Coke machines walking around and talking to me.

After a few short periods of sleep, I got up and started outlining a book *The Blizzard of the Millennium* which I would eventually finish. There would be a snow monster in the book that came from the Coke and Pepsi machines that had taunted me in my dreams.

About 17 inches of snow fell during that blizzard with 60 mile an hour winds to boot. The next day, in the afternoon, a neighbor made a path so I could get out of the school's parking lot and onto the plowed street. Amazingly, a kickball had been blown off the roof of our school, and it was setting next to a large drift in the back of my truck when I got out.

Yes, I replaced the meat and cheese trays. I tried to make ten free throws in a row many times during my time in the gym, but could only do nine. My runs through the hall were some of my favorite and most memorable ever. I could find only one radio station still on the air, country western, and I piped it through the halls while I was running.

Years later, I was doing an author visit in an Orlando, Florida school, in a pretty impoverished part of the city. Most of the kids there had never even seen snow. The kids were so attentive, almost transfixed, as I told them about the blizzard and writing the book. When I was done, a little boy yelled out, "No way that's true!"

I laughed as did many of the teachers, students, and parents in attendance. "Oh yes!" I said. "It's *all* true."

Story 12: Santa is Watching

My Aunt Eileen owned a ceramic shop named JK Creations, so I had a lot of great ceramic things all around my classroom, most of them painted by my mom and my sisters. There was a particularly large Santa in the back of the room on top of the cabinets, well out of reach of anyone.

Unknown to the kids, Santa had a little key chain next to him that made a repetitive musical sound whenever there was too much noise in the classroom. I'd purchased that when there weren't too many of them around, and when students asked me what that sound was, I'd reply, "I guess Santa thinks we're being too noisy."

I would also mention Santa a lot, saying things

like, "Please be quiet in the hall. Remember, Santa is watching!"

One time, things were disappearing from kids' desks—little things like special pens, key chains, rulers, etc. I had some suspicion about who was doing it, and when I did a weekend desk check, I figured out who it was. He had hidden one of the items under some other stuff in his desk. I took the item from his desk and put it back where it belonged.

Then I wrote a note on red paper that said, "Santa is watching!" I wrote it in a cursive handwriting—nothing like the printing I always used. I carefully placed it where he had placed the stolen item in his desk.

The next day, I waited until the student got to his desk and opened it up. I didn't look straight at him, but caught the expression in his eyes when he found the note. As he was reading it, the look in his eyes was amazing! Then he turned around and glanced up at Santa.

He never took anything more that year (that I know of) either.

Story 13: Describe That Guy That Just Came In

A policeman had recently visited my fifth grade class and answered numerous questions. One question and subsequent discussion fascinated me. It had to do with how difficult it is to get a good eye-witness description of someone that may have committed a crime.

I thought this might be a good writing lesson. One for my former students had an afternoon when he could come in after his last class in the afternoon. I told him to disguise himself as best as possible, wearing really wild, colorful stuff, then he would just walk around the classroom and leave.

As soon as he left, I had students take out pencil and paper and describe the person who had entered the room and left. Half an hour later, my former student came back in, still dressed up, and students read their descriptions.

The results were hilarious—and definitely proved the policeman's point. It is difficult to get an accurate description from eye witnesses. ... But at least everyone knew it wasn't a girl!

Story 14: Booger-Picker

I've had a hard time watching booger-picking. I had a teacher who picked his nose and then did really weird things with the boogers, so when I had a student that did this, I tried to break them of that habit with no embarrassment if possible.

This particular booger-picker student was seated in the back of one of the rows in the room. I had a private conference with him and told him that every time I noticed him going for a nasty nugget in his nose, I'd clear my throat and point my index finger toward my nose. If he broke the habit of booger-picking, we would go to TCBY Yogurt to celebrate.

It took a few months but it worked! TCBY and no more booger-picking!

Story 15: April Fools at Highland Acres

Highland Acres Elementary in Bismarck was a small school, grades one through six, just one classroom of each grade. Our principal, Mr. Fettig, thought it might be fun to see how kids would react if no one was around when they arrived on April Fools' Day.

All the teachers parked their cars away from the school, and the curtains in the staff room were pulled on the large windows looking onto the front of the school where we were hiding. The custodians and a few parents were around just to make sure safety wasn't an issue.

Well, when the bell rang, it didn't take long for things to start happening. In fact, a sixth grader in my class named Brad walked close to the window of the staff room where all of us could hear him clearly, and said to his friend, "This is probably Kremer's idea! Let's go home!"

We were out of the staff room in a hurry!

Story 16: Cross-Country Wrong Way!

I had so many gifted cross-country runners in my class over the years. They would compete in meets for fifth and sixth graders in the fall in Bismarck, mostly in parks and on golf courses. They had grit and determination that was inspirational!

By the time the last meet in October was held, the weather conditions could be pretty rough—cold and windy. On this particular October day, it was pretty cold and the wind was howling at the Tom O'Leary Golf Course in Bismarck. Three of us teachers were under a huge evergreen on the course, trying to get out of the cold wind as much as possible, waiting for all the runners to go by so we could give them encouragement.

One of the girls in my class was running against the wind, laughing as she went by us. "Hi, Dr. Kremer!" she said, fighting the wind.

Suddenly a big gust of wind caught her, and she was pushed backward for several moments—she was running *backward*!

"It's that way, Julie!" I yelled. "Run that way!"

She looked over at us under the tree and laughed as the wind died down, and she was able to run in the right direction again.

STORY 17: BAND-AID ON THE FACE

After I wrote the book *Are You Smarter than a Flying Gator* I did several author visits to elementary schools on the Space Coast of Florida one week, and each day I wore a Band-Aid on my face. I spoke to large groups of about 100-150 each time, and I waited to see if anyone would ask me why I had that small Band-Aid on my face.

Invariably, no matter what age group I was talking to, during the question–answer session after my presentation, someone would raise their hand and ask me why I was wearing the Band-Aid. Then I would have the person come up to the front of the room, and I would tell them that I was just curious if anyone would ask the question. After that, I would interview the person briefly, and eventually give them a signed book with a dollar bill as a bookmark.

STORY 18: THAT'S MY DADDY!

I visited lots of schools in Florida after finishing the book *Are You Smarter than a Flying Gator?* One school visit in the Pensacola area stands out. I knew from the time I entered the school that everyone was familiar with my writing. The halls were covered with kids' artwork from my books. I was treated like royalty, getting a nice polo shirt from the principal that I changed into and wore during the day. A retired colonel helped with the book signing in the afternoon in the library, and the kids ordered almost 500 books.

While I was speaking to a large group of students in the multipurpose room, I was showing them some of the funny artwork from the story, projecting it on a large screen. One of the illustrations featured the Blue Angels flying group from the United States Navy being led by a flying gator named Gator Mikey, the major character in my book.

A first grade girl yelled excitedly from the back of the room, "That's my **daddy**!"

Her daddy was the leader of the Blue Angels!

I said, "Wow! Would you please come up here!"

She smiled and came up to join me, not shy at all. I asked her some questions, and told her about how much I loved the Blue Angels, and even remembered them coming to Bismarck when I was about her age. Then I asked her for *her* autograph, and gave her an autographed book of mine. "And please tell your daddy how much I love the Blue Angels!" I added.

The girl had the biggest smile on her face.

Story 19: Hey! I wrote the book!

By this time I had written three books and had them published by Sweetgrass Publishing in Bismarck. It was always fun when one of my students read one of my books for reading class, and we had a conference about the book when they were done.

This particular time, a student had read my book *Saved by Custer's Ghost*, and we were discussing some of the aspects of the plot of the story. As the discussion continued, I was quite amazed and surprised when this boy started arguing with me about a particular portion of the plot.

I started laughing. Then I said something that I never dreamed I'd ever say in my life, "Hey Mark! I think I know something about the plot. I wrote the *book*!"

We both laughed.

Story 20: Most Surprising Teacher Christmas Gift

I'm guessing most teachers have received some interesting gifts at Christmas time, even some that were quite surprising. One gift stands out for me.

I was teaching in Bismarck at Highland Acres Elementary. The day before we got out for Christmas vacation, one of my students asked permission to leave the room. When he came back, he was carrying a black and white portable TV—certainly not the typical teacher Christmas gift.

I laughed—too surprised to say anything but … *What*!?

That gift would turn out to have special meaning in so many ways. The boy's mom turned out to be one of the best doctors in the world for my dad when he had heart and lung problems. I think she added 20 or more years to his life.

My mom used that TV for many years after that, and anytime I went to Mandan to visit, I was reminded of that gift and its significance.

Story 21: Bend down and Touch Your Ankles

Yes, this is all funny to me now, and I wouldn't trade these experiences and memories for anything. For me, noon hour at Mandan Junior High was fun and interesting. It meant running down to nearby Red Owl with some friends, buying a Ding Dong or Twinkie or other treat, eating it quickly, and running back in time for the Boys Choir that met during part of the noon hour. I recall we had about 20 minutes for our run to Red Owl and back.

Mr. Ernie Borr was the incredible choir director for our Boys Choir at Mandan Junior High. I loved the man, and we had all the respect in the world for him. He expected us to be on time, though, so we could maximize the 30 minutes or so we had each day to practice.

Well, my friends and I made it back on time all but once during those three years—and we knew what that meant. We had to bend down, touch our ankles, and feel the sting of the *board of education* on our backsides.

I still recall the lingering warmth on my backside that followed the *whack*.

Story 22: Half-Court Shot

I had a paper route right after school most of my first 12 school years, but I really wanted to play on the basketball team when I was a seventh grader. I was definitely a scrub, and our coach, Mr. Walters, put me in at the end of several games.

Our little, very old gym at Mandan Junior High was definitely a cracker box, but it had a lot of character. One time, at the end of a game where we trailed miserably, Mr. Walters sent me in for the last few minutes. I dribbled the ball, quite poorly by the way, just past the midcourt line and stopped. I looked at the basket, and I could feel it—so I took a shot. I knew it was good as soon as it left my hand. I could see the look on my coach's face as it slowly soared toward the basket. For just a moment, I was a little worried because I thought I may have launched the ball a little too hard ... but the ball eventually banked off the backboard and went in! I looked over at the bench. Coach Walters had a look on his face that told the story—pure astonishment and amazement and hilarity.

That one shot made my junior high basketball career worthwhile!

Story 23: Fake Seizure

Mr. Linder was teaching one of the Teacher Education courses at Jamestown College for upperclassmen who would eventually become teachers. I usually was the first one to show up for class, and Mr. Linder and I would often have good conversations.

One morning, he said, "Would you do something for me? I'd like to see how the class reacts when someone has a medical emergency. " He shared with me what he wanted me to do. "Let me start class, and after five minutes or so, fall straight forward out of your desk, and act like you're choking and having a seizure of some kind."

I said, "Okay."

After class had begun, Mr. Linder had spoken for about five minutes, I fell forward, tipping the desk over, and started shaking and choking. Instantly, several people came to my aid. One person had people stand back to give the others room. Then someone started loosening my belt, and Mr. Linder told them to stop.

"Okay, everyone!" Mr. Linder called out. "You can return to your desks. This was just a test."

Mr. Linder then explained what the two of us had done, how they had reacted, and he complimented them on their reactions.

It was amazing how fast news travels on a small college campus, and just how wrong it can be. At noon in the cafeteria I had to explain to several people that I was okay—and what had *really* happened.

Story 24: Look at Aunt Bertha

The Birthday Wheel started out as just a spinner from a board game, but eventually our school's awesome custodian built one that was as good as the one on *The Wheel of Fortune* but significantly smaller.

The Birthday Wheel had the numbers one through 10 on it. Here's how it worked. The numbers on the wheel corresponded to prizes. Some were good—like $3, a trip to A&B Pizza, a Camaro ride (in my 1976 Camaro), or a surprise package (A brown paper bag sealed with masking tape and loaded with fun stuff). Some of the prizes were not so good—like a can of hash, a hunk of head cheese, and a trip to the boiler room.

On their birthdays, kids would spin the birthday wheel keeping this in mind. The rules were—you could have up to three spins. If you didn't like the result of the first spin, you could go on to the second, and if you didn't like that, you could spin the wheel a third time. But if you chose to spin the birthday wheel that third time, you were stuck with the result.

Let's just say the Birthday Wheel resulted in lots of laughs over the years, but my favorite was when someone landed on seven on their third and final spin—and they were stuck with the result—go into the computer room with me, close the door, and stare at a photo of my Aunt Bertha. No one had ever gotten this result before. I went into the computer room, closed the door, and showed the student the photo of Aunt Bertha.

Aunt Bertha was a wonderful lady, but in her late 80's when this photo had been taken, she was quite a sight with her wig, makeup, and extra-dark red lipstick. When I showed the photo to this boy, he laughed. I whispered to him, "Everyone is going to want to know what it was like looking at this photo of Aunt Bertha. I'll give you a trip to Hardee's for your birthday if you give everyone a startled, frightened look when you leave this room—and maybe scream a little too."

He played the part so well. That's exactly what he did!

Story 25: All it takes is one word!

Sometimes, it's just one word that can make a particular class laugh the entire year. It could be my mispronunciation and exaggeration of one of the last names of one my awesome students that sets them off (Mueller becomes MUUUUEEELLER) or maybe it's a slightly exaggerated pronunciation of a vocabulary word like *lugubrious* (LOOO-GOOOOO-BREE-US), possibly it's a food that some North Dakotans love (head cheese or lutefisk).

Another one of my favorites was when we were studying science, and one of the girls in class said Yur-EEN for *urine*. After that, Yur-EEN became the funny word for that year. The word Yur-EEN would show up in many places, even in creative writing stories as the name of a pet or the name of a male or female character.

The word that was the most fun over the years, however, was the word *Hooooshka*. (My sister Jennifer married a Huschka and I changed the name *slightly*.) When I began writing books, the Hooooshkas became some of my favorite characters to write about. We even had a classroom character called the Hooooshkaman. One year the Hooooshkaman was featured on a T-shirt designed by one of my former students, Dave Ely.

Well, when I wrote my book *Santa's Our Substitute Teacher*, the Hooooshkas showed up again as characters that were pretty mean at the beginning of the book, but they redeemed themselves by the end. Anyway, kids of all ages loved that book. As I spoke to a school in Paisley, Florida, one little girl raised her hand and said, "My favorite part of your Santa book is the *Ho! Ho! HOOOOSHKA!* part at the end of the book."

I laughed and said, "I love that part too. It makes me laugh every time I think of it." ... Then I paused and said, "I wonder if all of you would say *Ho! Ho! HOOOOSHKA!* after I count to three. I'd like to hear ALL of you saying it at the same time. Ready? ... 1 ... 2 ... 3!"

"HO! HO! HOOOOSHKA!"

It was *amazing* to hear more than 300 people yell that at the same time. There was lots of laughter and smiles!

From that time on, I often finished my author visits with **HO! HO! HOOOOSHKA!**

Story 26: Behind the back

I always had things like little soft basketballs, baseballs, and footballs in the classroom, and with a few minutes left in the day, we'd play catch until the bell rang. I'd throw the ball underhand to each student and they would return it, and we would try to get all the way around the room without any drops. As the year progressed, the kids became really good at it. Sometimes we'd just keep going, and we'd go around the room more than once.

As my teaching career progressed, I started throwing it behind the back with my right hand, and eventually I became as good throwing it that way as doing it underhand. Well, one Halloween, there was a roll of toilet paper in the back of the room because we'd temporarily run out of

Kleenex. I grabbed the roll and we started playing catch. I threw it to each student, behind the back, and the students threw it back to me, as the roll of toilet paper slowly unraveled.

It was hilarious—and it became a Halloween tradition!

Story 27: Mathketball

Often when we were reviewing for a math test, I had a cool little basketball hoop that I would mount on the marker board in front of the class. Then students would try to answer a challenging math problem, and I'd have those who answered the problem correctly line up and take a shot at the basket from about 10 feet away.

Well, over the years, let's just say, many students became quite competitive. I found out that there were side bets going on with our classroom funny money behind my back, and some were comparing their proficiency at making baskets with mine.

Recently, one student, now almost 50, tracked me down on Facebook. His first message to me was, "Remember how I beat you by one basket for the whole year in mathketball?"

This kid was an excellent athlete and I responded to him, "Actually, no, but I remember how good you were at mathketball, and I don't doubt it!"

Story 28: Math Football Game

My first year of teaching was in Rugby, North Dakota. From the beginning of the year, we played a math football game. It had all the elements of a real football game using spinners and dice plus a realistic football field drawn on the front chalkboard and a small football marking the progress of the offensive team. The kids loved it!

During the football season that year we often played the math football game on Fridays, matching the Rugby High School Football Team against the football team that would be their opponent that night. Then I'd go to the games, and many of the 75 fifth graders I taught math would be at the game too.

Well, what happened became funny, but a little creepy. The final results of the first three math football games we played in class were eerily close to the final results of the actual high school games. The same team that had won our math football game also won the high school football game, and the scores were really close too. I started getting a lot of glances from kids and parents in the crowd during the games.

That trend continued the entire season, with only one exception—and that Math Football Game became one of my favorite classroom activities.

Story 29: Money Tree

I had an amazing class this particular year. I almost hated to leave them at all, but I'd accumulated five days of personal leave, and I wanted to use those days to go on a cruise during February, the coldest part of the year in North Dakota.

Before I left, one of the parents carried in a small dead tree with no leaves—with currency from my class that was attached to each of the branches for me to use on my trip. It made me laugh and almost cry—and it also paid for all the adult beverages and T-shirts I bought on the cruise!

Story 30: Poolside Party

Some of my fondest school memories involve the school celebrations at the end of the year. When

I was going to elementary school in Mandan, we had some great picnics at Riverside Park that still appear in my dreams. I loved playing *drop-the-stick-got it* on the merry-go-round and eating burnt hot dogs. As a teacher, roller skating and bowling parties and trips to the Super Slide Amusement Park in Bismarck stand out.

But one party for my students makes me laugh, and it was the most fun of all. We basically had the pool area and hot tub at the beautiful Kirkwood Motor Inn in Bismarck all to ourselves for an afternoon. We also had two rooms for the kids to get snacks, use the bathroom, etc.

My brother and sister, Kelly and Jennifer, both lifeguards, watched over the action in the pool for me. Several parents stayed around, but there was absolutely no discipline needed at all. It was pure *fun*—and it still makes me laugh to see the faces of the students when they saw the bathtubs full of ice and cans of pop and the large boxes full of snacks in bags.

The funniest thing of all might have been when there were so many kids in the large hot tub, the water level went right to the top, just about ready to overflow. Then they asked me to join them. I got in very slowly, and everyone laughed as it started to overflow!

Story 31: It's Polka Time

It was the night before the last day of school my first year of teaching. Thanks to the other two fifth grade teachers in Rugby, North Dakota, both with more than 20 years of teaching experience, I had a fantastic first year of teaching. They had coached me all year.

Well, these ladies wanted to have a little celebration at a bar in nearby Knox the night before the last day of school, and I couldn't turn that down. But I had no idea what I was getting into! Let's just say—way too many adult beverages—and way too much polka-dancing—something I had never done before.

I had a hangover you wouldn't believe that next day—the last day of school for the year. Thank goodness the afternoon was spent outdoors!

Story 32: The Ghost Radio in the Gym

This is really funny now, but it wasn't so funny

back then. At certain times when I was in the gym, there seemed to be a radio playing somewhere above the ceiling tiles. I knew it had nothing to do with the intercom in the school, and when I asked our custodian about it, he told me some construction workers might have left the radio in the gymnasium ceiling during construction of Dorothy Moses Elementary School.

That made little sense to me. That was many years ago! And wouldn't the batteries have run down long ago? Also, the radio seemed to go on at the strangest times, and it wasn't always playing the same genre of music either.

Well, one night I was in the school all by myself. I decided I was going to go down to the gym and shoot a few baskets before going home. About twenty minutes into it, the ghost radio went on, playing rock music.

You probably have experienced that spine-tingling thing that goes up your back at certain times!? "I'm *outta* here!" I yelled up at the radio.

Story 33: Comedy Relief at the Formal School Evaluation

Dorothy Moses School was going through an extensive evaluation process with lots of visitors examining every part of our school during this particular week. It put a lot of pressure on everyone in the school, but the process seemed to be going really well.

On the evening of the evaluators' last day in the school, our principal, Mr. Fettig, decided to have a get-together in our gym where evaluators could unwind with Dorothy Moses teachers and staff, and everyone could enjoy some good food. It would also give some of the evaluators a chance to make some comments—plus we had a little *surprise* for them.

The atmosphere in the gym was pretty light as we started eating, but it still felt a little too serious. Our principal asked me to be the master of ceremonies, so I got up behind a podium and thanked everyone, and then made a few friendly comments. Then I seriously told everyone that one of the most experienced teachers at our school had a few things he wanted to tell the evaluators about the school before they finished their work. I introduced our longtime phy. ed. teacher, Mr.

Jim Birkholz, as someone who probably knew as much about our school as anyone. Then Jim walked up to the podium, looking very serious.

From the first word he spoke, it didn't sound good. Jim Birkholz was talking about how *he didn't get any respect* in the school. He started naming some names ... starting with our principal ... it was getting uncomfortable. But it didn't take long for people to realize he was doing an imitation of Rodney Dangerfield, a comedian who was very popular at the time. People were soon laughing hysterically. I was laughing so hard, I was crying.

I still laugh when I think about the looks on those evaluators' faces!

Story 34: My First "B" Ever

I was in Mr. Reisenhauer's seventh grade geography class at Mandan Junior High School. As the year progressed, I *pretty much* figured out all the questions he would ask on his challenging tests before he handed them out. It was a little game I played to prepare myself for his tests.

Well, I had a chance to prove my point. My

brother Mike had just won a small, cheap, reel-to-reel tape recorder by getting the most people to subscribe to our local newspaper. This was a time, in the early 60's, when cheap reel-to-reel tape recorders were pretty rare. The quality of the sound of Mike's new recorder was pretty good, and it gave me an idea.

I went to Mr. Reisenhauer and said, "My Reisenhauer, I think I can predict what most of your questions are going to be on your next test. What if I put all the questions and answers for the test on a tape recorder, and I'll give it to you when you pass out the test so you can see how good I do."

He thought about it a few seconds, laughed, and said, "Let's do one better. I'll let you play the entire tape to the class before the test. I suspect it might benefit some of the other kids as a good review for the test."

I was pleasantly surprised, and I couldn't wait to prove my point.

When Mr. Reisenhauer played my tape before the test, it was interesting watching his face. I had a feeling I'd done a good job, but I'd soon find out.

After the test was passed out, some students started giggling. As everyone was working on the test, Mr. Reisenhauer seemed to be enjoying himself too. Let's just say—I'd nailed it!

Later the next day, I was walking to another class, when someone called my name.

"Hey Kremer!"

I turned around, and one of the biggest troublemakers in the school was staring me in the face. I knew he had flunked at least one grade, and I heard he beat up a lot of kids too. He was referred to as a *hood* back then, and I avoided him like I avoided the green vegetables in the cafeteria.

"Thanks, Kremer!" he said. "That's the first 'B' I ever got!"

I didn't ask him if he meant the first "B" in that class or the first "B" *ever*, but it sure made me feel good.

Story 35: Kremer Kash

Most of my students called it Kremer Kash and some called it Funny Money, but it definitely had real value. It was the currency in the classroom with denominations 1, 2, 5, 10, 50, 100, and 500, with each denomination on a different color paper.

At first I designed it, but then I had a student named Jan Pedersen (now Dr. Jan Jones, M.D.) do it. She had the creative ability to create Kremer Kash with all sorts of funny tidbits and phrases and artwork on it. To me, Jan's funny money was a masterpiece! She continued to design the Kremer Kash for years.

Students could earn funny money a variety of ways—through good behavior, good grades, good predicting of football games, good reading, good attendance, etc. The money had value because it was used at auctions throughout the year—mostly on Halloween, Valentine's Day, and the last week of school.

Well, as time went on I carried a 100 dollar bill of funny money in my pocket, just in case a former student was working as a cashier at a grocery store, Target, or some other place in Bismarck.

When it happened, I'd have them check out the items I was buying, then I'd slap the $100 bill of Kremer Kash on the counter and say, "Keep the change!"

Story 36: Peanut Butter Sandwiches

One of my favorite writing activities involved students having to write an accurate description of how to make a peanut butter sandwich. Before they began, I pointed to the jar of peanut butter, the closed sack of bread, and the butter knife in front of me on a desk. I told them to be *very specific* in their written directions.

The very first time I did this, the first person who volunteered to read his directions turned out to be the perfect person to illustrate how challenging writing good directions can be. His very first sentence "First, put the peanut butter on the bread!"—and I placed the jar of peanut butter on the sack of bread.

It got much worse after that! Before we were done, I had bread and peanut butter all over and everyone was laughing!

Story 37: Scavenger Hunt in Rugby

My first year of teaching, there were a lot of first-year and young teachers in the Rugby School District. One of them was particularly fun-loving, and she organized a Halloween scavenger hunt around Rugby followed by a party at her house.

We were put into groups of five for the scavenger hunt. It was a fun, challenging event, and the clues took us all over the Rugby area. Well, one of the clues took us to the cemetery, to a particular gravesite. Our group drove into the cemetery in the dark, and two of us ran over to the gravesite to retrieve the clue. All of a sudden, at least three spotlights were shined on us from several police vehicles! We looked around the well-lit area around us, and were shocked to see several gravestones had been tipped over around where we were standing!

We ended up at the police station and told our story, but a policeman still called the superintendent of schools, who fortunately vouched for us. We had a great time at the party later, and had a funny story to tell after that.

Story 38: Rhyme all the Time

It was a little annoying at first—then it got to be fun—then I started to do it myself. This student in my class named Brent rhymed all the time. I'm not sure when he started rhyming that year, but I think it was the first week of school. It started out with answers to questions I'd ask, like, "What are the common nouns in that sentence?"

He would answer with something like, "The common nouns are nurse and *hat*—what do you think of *that*?"

Well, let's just say the creative writing stories had a LOT of rhyming in them that year. And when I started writing books, Brent became a major character—the kid who rhymed all the time.

Story 39: The Band-Aid Class

I used up the classroom supply, then I needed to buy some more at Target. The Band-Aid class always seemed to need Band-Aids. I ran out of the school brand and ended up buying more fashionable ones.

Then they asked for *more* Band-Aids—then they

were wearing Band-Aids when they didn't need Band-Aids. Then I was wearing Band-Aids.

Story 40: I Think That's Larry Bird!

What were the chances? I was on my way to Hawaii with my good friend, sixth grade teacher Duane Roth. We were looking forward to a whole week in Hawaii during the coldest part of the school year in North Dakota.

We had to change flights at the Minneapolis Airport early in the morning. As we were walking down the hall, I couldn't believe it! That was Larry Bird walking with two other Boston Celtic greats about 50 yards away in front of us!

I had a book in my hand, the one I was reading to my fifth grade class, and I asked Duane excitedly, "Do you have a pen? I've got to get their autographs!"

Duane handed his pen to me, and I ran down the hall and caught up with Larry Bird, Robert Parish, and Kevin McHale. They'd just lost a game to the Minnesota Timberwolves, and it was early in the morning, but I approached them with a big smile on my face.

"I'm so sorry to bother you guys," I said, my heart beating through my chest. "You are my favorite basketball players *ever*, and I've been watching you since your college days—would you mind autographing this book for me? My fifth graders aren't going to believe this!"

The three couldn't have been nicer to me considering the circumstances. Later, I put the autograph of Larry Bird on the back of our classroom T-shirts for that year.

STORY 41: 50 BELOW! NO PROBLEM!

This group of fifth graders was so much fun! They were smart, creative, and I never knew what to expect each day and I loved it! Playing kickball outside as a class on Friday afternoons was a tradition, and this group of fifth graders was determined to play kickball *every* Friday afternoon, no matter what the weather conditions.

One Friday, though, it was 50 below wind chill, with lots of snow on the ground, and it had been announced in the morning that no one was to go out at all. Well, that didn't stop this group. Two of the girls volunteered to plead our case with the principal. Once they came back with the okay, four boys asked to go out and shovel the base paths so we could run around them.

Well, we played kickball that afternoon, and it was as much fun as we'd ever had! I still remember the many laughs as they dove into the snow to catch a ball.

Story 42: Mr. Bubble Visits

One of the greatest men I ever met was Harold Schafer. He had invented things like Mr. Bubble bubble bath and Glass Wax. He had also done so much for the state of North Dakota, including turning Medora into a world class tourist destination.

Mr. Schafer also did many great things for many people, including me. As I traveled to 49 states, I ran into several other people along the way whose lives had been touched by Harold Schafer.

One day I was telling my students about Mr. Schafer, and one of them asked, "Do you think you could ask him to visit our class?"

By this time, he was in his early 80s, I think, but I told my class I'd give it a try. When I tried to call him later, I got right through, and he asked me when I would like to have him come in.

It was a thrill to have Harold Schafer visit with my students and me. But we got a good chuckle on the morning of his visit when a student asked, "When is Mr. Bubble coming?"

STORY 43: STEELERS FAN FOR LIFE

I'm a die-hard STEELERS fan, and many of my students were fans of other teams. I did everything I could to change that.

Several years I would tell them, "I'll give you a choice of a Terrible Towel or a Steelers keychain, but you've got to promise you'll become a STEELERS fan for life.

Several decades later—many of them are still STEELERS fans!

Story 44: Upside-Down Argument

One of the most precocious kids I ever had when I was teaching sixth grade liked to argue about subjects that were a little off topic as often as possible, and many times it was fun. Sometimes—not so much.

One day I wasn't in the mood at all, but Mike decided to proceed anyway. "Mike! Do you think you could continue your argument upside-down?"

"What do you mean?" Mike asked me.

"I'd like to see you arguing upside-down," I replied.

Not long after that, he was hanging upside-down, me holding him by his ankles. You guessed it, he just kept on talking. And I kept arguing with him. Mike was a pretty big sixth grader and it required every ounce of strength I had and a little more. My weightlifting had definitely paid off.

Several weeks later Mike's mom and dad came to the parent-teacher conference. His dad said, "I can't believe you were able to lift Mike upside-down like that! There's no way I could do that!"

Story 45: Can't You Even Beat My Student Manager?

Legendary football and track coach Rollie Greeno was also the physical education teacher for the freshmen at Jamestown College (now the University of Jamestown). One of the first activities my freshman year was running up the 300-yard hill. That involved running up the street adjacent to the football field and behind Watson Hall. It was pretty challenging.

I had to run that hill with two freshmen that Coach Greeno had recruited for track, and I beat both of them. I was attending the school with academic scholarships and making a little money on work-study filming athletic contests, cleaning wrestling mats, and doing anything else Coach Greeno wanted me to do. (He even had me shovel around the track on a very cold day one time so he could jog.)

Anyway, Coach Greeno was not too happy when I beat his track recruits that day. He yelled, "What the h-ll!? You two guys are going to be on my track team, and you can't even beat one of my student managers!?"

Story 46: Most Embarrassing Junior High Memory

You probably remember at least one embarrassing moment from junior high. I have one that's funny now, but it wasn't so funny then—until the day was over. I was reminded of it when I was watching quarterback Tom Brady rip a seam on the rear-end area of his pants during the golf event with Michelson, Woods, and Peyton Manning when they were raising money for COVID-19 relief.

Back when I went to school, Mandan Junior High consisted of grades 7-9. I had a paper route and was able to buy some pretty nice clothes at the men's store in town named Greengard's. The pants were a little tight, though, and I ripped them the same place as Tom Brady as I was getting into one of those uncomfortable desks from the 60s. Now what? I certainly wasn't going to the office to ask to go home and change. That wasn't even in my thoughts. Thank goodness sweaters were in vogue, and the one I was wearing was long enough to cover things up pretty well.

That day went *really* slow. Just about every time I moved, I carefully pulled my sweater down, hoping to cover up my rear-end seam rip.

Somehow, I got through the day without anyone pointing out the embarrassing split.

Story 47: Three Johns

Teachers have special challenges when there are two students with the same first name in the classroom, but early in my teaching career, I had *three Johns*. They were all great kids, and I hated using their last initial when calling out their names—John L., John R., and John S.

I decided to just say *John!*—*extra-loud*, (remember NORM! from the TV show *Cheers*? It was a lot like that.) and let them all respond.

John!

It was a guilty pleasure to see all three *Johns* respond so willingly and enthusiastically.

Story 48: Uncle Jack

I've done many author visits, but the one I did to Anna Maria Island north of Sarasota stands out for several reasons.

I usually show up about an hour early for my

visits to make sure everything has been set up the way I requested. When I got to Anna Maria Island, their multi-purpose room was a mess from a group that had met there the night before, so the custodian and I vacuumed it quickly. ... Whatever it takes!

The next surprise came from the cutest first grade twin boys you've ever seen. During the question-answer session of my author visit, they told me how much they liked the book. I looked at them and smiled, "There's no way you two read that book! It's written at about the seventh grade reading level!"

"Yes, we did," one of them replied.

Their teacher was sitting nearby and she was nodding her head, indicating that she knew they had.

"Come on up here, you two. I want to ask you a few questions about the book, just to make sure."

They came up to the front, and everyone applauded. Then I started asking them questions to test their comprehension. They answered every one perfectly.

The last thing that happened was awesome. I was talking about my favorite character, and I mentioned the amazing dolphin in the story, Jack Lambert. In reality Jack Lambert is my favorite football player of all-time, #58 from the Pittsburgh Steelers.

I got a HUGE surprise when a little girl raised her hand and said, "My uncle is Jack Lambert!"

"What!?" I said incredulously. "No WAY! Your Uncle Jack Lambert is my favorite football player of all-time!"

I then asked her to come up and join me on stage, and I interviewed her, got her autograph, and gave her a book to give to her Uncle Jack.

49: No way, Jamie!

Jamie Martinson was one of my super-students my first year of teaching sixth grade at Highland Acres Elementary in Bismarck. One day he brought a box to school and put it on my desk. "This is for you," he said.

I opened it up, and there were the two cutest baby sheltie collies in the world in the box, part of the litter from his family's two collies. One was a girl, and the smaller one was a boy. As you might imagine, the whole class couldn't believe how cute they were.

"They might be the cutest things I've ever seen," I told Jamie, "but you know I can't have pets in my apartment."

"Oh, I know that," Jamie replied, "but you have your younger brothers and sisters and mom and dad in Mandan. I want you to take them to them. If they keep them, you will be able to enjoy them too."

I laughed. "Jamie, my dad never allowed pets in the house, except maybe goldfish. Now my dad has some allergy issues too, so there's no chance they will be able to keep a collie—and surely not *two*."

Jamie was persistent. "Well, maybe we can go over there after school and see what they say."

That's what we did. Amazingly, my dad totally fell in love with both dogs—even more than my brothers and sisters! They almost kept them both, but finally they decided to pick the smaller boy sheltie, and they named him *Jamie*.

Jamie became best buddies with my dad, and best friends to all of us. He was with us 17 years, and he was the major character in my first book, *A Kremer Christmas Miracle*.

50. Kevin # 1 and Kevin # 2

It still makes me laugh.

"I'd like to run with you on your birthday and buy you breakfast afterwards."

"What!?" I chuckled when Kevin Feeney asked me this question in late November when he was in my sixth grade class. This had certainly never happened before—one of my students wanted to get up *really* early in the morning on a cold day on my birthday and run six miles in the dark, probably on a slippery course, and then buy me breakfast! How could I turn that down?

I said, "As you know, Kevin, I run six miles at about 4:00 a.m. so I can get to school early. Are you sure you want to do that?"

"Yes."

I wasn't about to question Kevin any more. He was one of the most determined kids I'd ever had in class, and he was also a *Kevin*. I'd actually first met Kevin when he was a first grader, shooting baskets by himself outside the school on a cold winter day on the weekend. At that time, I'd asked him if he wanted to come in the school and warm up, and he just smiled and said, "No, I'm plenty warm, but thanks, Dr. Kremer."

Well, that early morning run with Kevin turned out to be fantastic, and the breakfast afterward was awesome too. I couldn't believe how Kevin kept up the whole time on the run at a conversational pace on a course that was a little slushy and slippery—a beautiful course that included running over two bridges spanning the Missouri River.

Later, I would follow the life of Kevin Feeney all the rest of his way through school. I even got to watch many of his high school football games from the top of the press box with Kevin's amazing mom, Jan Feeney, who was filming the games. From up there, I got the greatest view of the games as I charted the Bismarck Demons' pass plays and put them on a separate video tape for Coach Bob Feeney, one of the all-time great coaches in North Dakota history.

After that, Kevin was so much fun to watch as he played quarterback for the Bison of North Dakota State before beginning his brilliant high school coaching career in North Dakota and then moving on to Moorhead, Minnesota, where he still coaches. I've also been lucky to meet the whole Feeney Clan when they've come to Florida.

For years, Kevin Feeney called me Kevin # 1, and he was Kevin # 2. That always made me smile.

About the Author

Kevin Kremer loved math in school, and he never dreamed he would become a writer. When he started teaching, he began writing stories with his fifth graders, and he loved it. His first published book, *A Kremer Christmas Miracle*, was actually a Christmas gift to his fifth graders.

Kremer grew up in Mandan, North Dakota, and he loves to write books involving that area. He also likes to include his favorite places in Mandan in his writing—including Ohm's Cafe and A&B Pizza.

Dr. Kremer has written, edited, and published more than 100 books, and he loves writing children's books the most. Kremer also likes helping other authors with challenges they are having with their own book projects.

Kremer has a writing-publishing company to help people with book projects of any kind. To contact him regarding book or e-book projects, school author visits, or to purchase books, go to:

Web site: **KevinKremerBooks.com**

E-mail: **snowinsarasota@aol.com**

Facebook: **Kevin Kremer Books**

To arrange for a reasonably priced author visit or to buy other great books go to:
KevinKremerBooks.com

Published by Kremer Publishing
2020
P.O. Box 1385
Osprey, FL 34229-1385
(941) 822-0549

www.ingramcontent.com/pod-product-compliance
Lightning Source LLC
Chambersburg PA
CBHW071306110426
42743CB00042B/1189